THE 10 RULES OF ROCK AND ROLL

THE 10 RULES OF ROCK AND ROLL

Collected Music Writings 2005-11

Robert Forster

The 10 Rules of Rock and Roll

Collected Music Writings 2005–11

Robert Forster

A Jawbone book
Revised and updated edition 2011
Published in the UK and the USA by Jawbone Press
2a Union Court,
20–22 Union Road,
London SW4 6JP,
England
www.jawbonepress.com

This edition published by permission of Foruli Ltd, London, England
www.foruli.co.uk

ISBN 978-1-906002-91-6

EDITOR: Thomas Jerome Seabrook
DESIGN: Paul Cooper Design

Printed by Regent Publishing Services Limited, China.

1 2 3 4 5 15 14 13 12 11

CONTENTS

BOOKS

CONCERTS

ON GRANT

OTHER WRITINGS

FICTION

To Karin
Who always believed

Introduction, or How I Became a Rock Critic

Seven years ago this book was not on the horizon. Then I was one of two singer–songwriters in The Go-Betweens and we had just completed our ninth album, *Oceans Apart*, in London. It was before Christmas 2004 when the band's Australian manager, Bernard Galbally, phoned to tell me that the editor of a new magazine, to be called *The Monthly*, was enquiring to see if I was interested in being its rock critic.

The editor was Christian Ryan. He was someone I didn't know, and the fact that I couldn't see or hold the magazine he was putting together added to the difficulty of the decision I had to make. My involvement required a leap of faith and the leap was going to be made in the public eye. But I could also see the confidence he was showing in me: my entire published writings, my portfolio so to speak, consisted of an article I'd written on hair care for a Manchester fanzine called *Debris* back in 1987, and a review of a Bob Dylan album in the German rock magazine *Spex* in 1990. Whatever had prompted Christian Ryan to invite me to write for *The Monthly*, I knew it couldn't have been what I'd done so far; it must have been based on what he thought I could do – which was intriguing and flattering to me.

I told Bernard I would think on it over Christmas. The other stumbling block was that I knew of no other practising rock musician in the world writing regular published music criticism. Linked to this was the ancient divide, not too strong in my mind, between journalists on one side of the fence with their pens and supposed frustrated rock-star dreams, and the bourbon-drinking, cigarette-puffing, 'they don't understand us' world of the musicians on the other. In the end the decision to say yes was relatively simple. When had following the dictates of rock 'n' roll lore ever had anything to do with me? And when I spoke to Christian Ryan, he dropped one important piece of information. He told me that Helen Garner was going to be the film critic. Then I knew. Then the scale and ambition of *The Monthly* became clear, as did the twist and angle that Christian wanted from his writers in relation to the subjects they were going to review.

One thing, though. Helen Garner had novels, screenplays and much published journalism behind her. I had *Spex* and the aptly named *Debris*, and the words 'deadline' and 'line editor' were only familiar from movies such as *All the President's Men*. So a plan was hatched. I'd write 1500 words on any new record I wished, send it to Christian, who was to be my editor, and if what I wrote failed – total honesty being a part of our pact – then we'd end our experiment with no one the wiser, and he would engage a writer with a more conventional past in rock criticism.

Two pieces of good fortune then interceded. Firstly, the release of *Oceans Apart* was underway, and with the band's other songwriter, Grant McLennan, I found myself in Amsterdam on a European promotional tour, where I snared an early copy of what was to be that year's hot album: Antony and the Johnsons' *I Am a Bird Now*. And secondly, back in Brisbane I found that I could write paragraph after paragraph of my feelings and thoughts about this record without tripping up. I didn't know if what I wrote was good, or whether it would be accepted, the review beginning with the narrative of my listening to the album while sitting in the back of a taxi in Milan traffic, and not with a plotted course of the history of Antony and the Johnsons.

So the big thank you of this introduction goes out to Christian Ryan; for not only thinking sideways and then taking the gamble of hiring me, but also for his stewardship of my career as music critic, which started with his wonderfully enthusiastic response to my first review and the fine editing and advice he brought to my work. This book would not have been written without him.

Christian left *The Monthly* after six months, and without wishing to be flippant, this may not have been as traumatic for Helen Garner or Clive James or any other of the seasoned contributors as it was for me. Christian was the only editor I'd ever known. I was worried how I was going to go with the new regime, both technically and on a personal level. I needn't have been: Sally Warhaft, the new editor, was instantly reassuring, enthusiastic and very capable, and with her came David Winter, my new line editor. David's editing skills are evident in most of *The Monthly* articles in this volume and I thank him and Sally for helping me develop as a writer in tandem with the growth and maturity they both brought to the magazine. Since their departure I have begun a good working relationship with *The Monthly*'s most recent editor, Ben Naparstek, which I look forward to continuing.

I am very happy to see this updated and revised version of *The 10 Rules of Rock and Roll* on Jawbone Press. For this edition of the book I have added five new reviews from 2010 and one from 2011. To further refine the content I have withdrawn three reviews that had a particularly Australian bias, and concentrated, when I can, on more internationally known artists in the new inclusions.

I remain writing at *The Monthly*, enjoying the support of the editorial team. The magazine in its sixth year, is successful, and I continue to discover music of interest and just as importantly continue to be intrigued by the people who make it.

Robert Forster, *Brisbane, April 2011*

The 10 Rules of Rock and Roll

1. Never follow an artist who describes his or her work as 'dark'.
2. The second-last song on every album is the weakest.
3. Great bands tend to look alike.
4. Being a rock star is a 24-hour-a-day job.
5. The band with the most tattoos has the worst songs.
6. No band does anything new on stage after the first 20 minutes.
7. The guitarist who changes guitars on stage after every third number is showing you his guitar collection.
8. Every great artist hides behind their manager.
9. Great bands don't have members making solo albums.
10. The three-piece band is the purest form of rock and roll expression.

ALBUMS

The Return of the Wichita Lineman

Glen Campbell's *Meet Glen Campbell*

Put yourself in Glen Campbell's shoes. You're 72. You've sold 45 million records. You've been married four times, most recently back in 1982. You have eight children. Your time is spent primarily on the golf course – there was the Glen Campbell Los Angeles Open on the pro-golf circuit through the '70s. You smoke cigars and you belong to the Messianic Judaism movement. You haven't made a charting pop record for 30 years, though you play the odd gig or tour and occasionally a live record or a selection of Christian songs comes out under your name. And of course you live in Malibu. Then this long-haired guy comes to one of your shows and tells you he's a record producer, and he not only wants to make a record with you of songs written mostly by young people you've never heard of, but he's also approached your old record label, Capitol – the one you had your big hits with back in the '60s, like 'Galveston', 'Gentle on My Mind', 'By the Time I Get to Phoenix' – and they're enthusiastic about the idea. They want you back. As you stand in your dressing room, guitar around your neck, stage sweat on your brow, you'd have to ask yourself: Do I really want to go through this one more time?

The old performer approached by the young producer raised and forever seared by the old performer's peak early work has become something of a show-business staple. The White Stripes' Jack White produced a great album, *Van Lear Rose* (2004) for Loretta Lynn. Karma County's Brendan Gallagher, with a bunch of fresh songs by artists ranging from The Reels to Ed Kuepper, made *Messenger* (1999) a hit album for Jimmy Little. The granddaddy of all these stories is the Rick Rubin and Johnny Cash hook-up in the mid '90s. It began in a similar fashion to Glen Campbell and his producer, Julian Raymond – with a backstage meeting – and resulted in a multi-album twilight-of-life renaissance for Cash. Since then, the term 'Rick Rubinise' has entered the rock-music lexicon. And on first glance, this seems to be the case with *Meet Glen Campbell*. There are the bizarre cover-song choices – Cash did Nine Inch Nails and Soundgarden; Campbell does Foo Fighters and Green Day – and there is the producer's mission to remind the artist of the qualities that made him great in the first place. But Glen Campbell is no Johnny Cash, and Raymond, though obviously acknowledging the Rubin blueprint, is moving Campbell in a different direction. The resulting album is less an older man squinting at death and time, and more a 72-year-old in rude health effortlessly making a great pop record.

It's easy to forget just how good Glen Campbell once was. Because he wasn't a singer–songwriter in a golden age of singer–songwriters, and his best work was done in a relatively short time and long ago, he has tended to be pushed to the back of the mind. Before he was a pop star he was one of the best session guitarists in LA, playing on everything from 'You've Lost That Lovin' Feelin'' to 'I'm a Believer' via Sinatra's 'Strangers in the Night'. He was also in The Beach Boys for a year as Brian Wilson's tour replacement, and he played on their masterpiece, *Pet Sounds* (1966). This would all be enough to garner him a place (albeit a footnote) in rock history, without the string of extraordinary songs he took to the charts at the tail end of the '60s. 'Wichita Lineman', 'By the Time I Get to Phoenix' and 'Galveston' had something that immediately lifted them out of the cheesy pop pack. These moody, mostly chorusless songs, with their weird narratives, searing strings and twangy guitar, went beyond 'teen' and hit another level. It was drama-laden pop music. The songs of maverick songwriter Jimmy Webb in the hands of a thirty-something singer–guitarist – this wasn't a sure-fire pop formula. But that's what made it great and has held the songs to the heart of golden-oldies radio, and to the pop ear, ever since.

Raymond has created a sound that blends Campbell old with Campbell new. It is difficult to bridge contemporary West-Coast production and the sensitivity and oddball elements of vintage Campbell. But it works. The strings and the ringing guitar lines are melded into a thicker, rockier sound. Raymond is helped in this transition by the sheer strength and beauty of Campbell's voice. Rubin had to tread carefully around an obviously older and at times failing Cash. Neil Diamond, who has also had Rubin at the helm on his latest albums, had his frailties exposed. Campbell roars. His singing is amazing, and Raymond confidently places him slap-bang in the centre of every mix. It's a 72-year-old sounding like a 40-year-old, and there isn't a glitch or a hint of fatigue. Besides the shock of the song selection – and there is a Velvet Underground song covered here – the force and quality of the singing is what marks this album.

The record starts with a hit, and if there was any justice in the world, Glen Campbell belting out Travis's 'Sing' would be coming from every radio right now. And by hit, I don't mean it's good and melodic and wouldn't it be nice. I mean, this has got muscle and hooks and fairy dust all over it, and it deserves to sit beside Madonna and The Veronicas and be programmed by the big FM-radio conglomerates. As the first track, it also sends the message that Campbell will fulfil the album's brief: a wide-ranging and interesting song cycle made with absolute conviction and craft. Song selection is where this album could have fallen down, but none of the choices – be it The Replacements' 'Sadly Beautiful' or Jackson Browne's 'These Days' or Green Day's 'Good Riddance (Time of

Your Life)' – sounds kooky or gimmicky. Campbell and Raymond 'get' every one. There is the tingle that comes with the realisation that Glen Campbell is actually singing 'Jesus' by The Velvet Underground or 'Times Like These' by Foo Fighters, but that soon yields to relief and at times wonder that Campbell can so comfortably get under the skin of these songs.

Some of the numbers set up interesting juxtapositions. 'These Days' by Jackson Browne is the quintessential mid-to-late-'60s finger-picked folk song ("I've been out walking / I don't do too much talking these days"), written by Browne when he was still in his teens. The lyric has a weariness and noble resignation well beyond the writer's tender years. It was first recorded by Nico, whom Browne was accompanying on guitar in Greenwich Village when she was collecting songs for her first solo album, *Chelsea Girl* (1967). Nico wrings every piece of Weltschmerz she can out of it, and her dark, low voice and bleak Teutonic world view emphasise the song's existential stoicism. In the hands of Campbell, 40 years later, it gains another meaning. Here is a man looking back at life, reading the wrong turns and decisions with a resigned, almost wistful tone. The lyric neatly passes through three generations – the teenage songwriter, the 30-year-old Bohemian princess, the aged Californian legend – and each takes something of their own from this lovely song.

And that's the surprise: for an artist regarded as lightweight and a singer of other people's songs, there is a biography in this album. Admittedly, it may help to know a little of Campbell's life, but the sequencing of the ten songs and the correlation between their stories and even a rough outline of the singer's story seems to confirm it, and gives the album a cohesion and depth that perhaps no other Glen Campbell album has had. There are love songs: hard-fought-for and treasured love – "I can only thank God it was not too late" – on Tom Petty's 'Angel Dream'. There are children left behind, achingly articulated on 'Sadly Beautiful'. And then there is 'Jesus'. Any irony Lou Reed may have packed into this song back in the dark days of The Velvet Underground, in late-'60s New York, is blown away by Campbell's straight and needy reading. The album closes on Lennon and Ono's 'Grow Old with Me'; with its chiming chorus, "God bless our love", its appeal to Campbell is obvious. It is the one shaky choice on the album, but given the quality of what has come before it is hard to deny Campbell his walk off into the sunset.

We are in the sixth decade of rock 'n' roll, so the unexpected, and the fact that it is being done by rock's senior citizens, should come as no revelation. What is interesting is that Glen Campbell joins another middle-of-the-roader, Neil Diamond, in the search for new horizons, while the old rebels – the Stones, The Who – are bogged and scared. Perhaps Campbell was meant to last. Two lines from 'These Days', which falls at the halfway point of the album, ring in the mind. Campbell sings them slowly, and with great care and beauty. "Please don't confront me with my failures / I had not forgotten them." It's as if he did the whole record just to get that out.

Seeing the Light

Bonnie 'Prince' Billy's *Lie Down in the Light*

There are cult stars and then there are cult stars. Will Oldham, born in Louisville, Kentucky, in 1970, is one of the great enigmas of music. His first five records, appearing from 1993 onwards, were released under variations on the Palace moniker – Palace Brothers, Palace Songs and Palace Music – and established him as a talent and someone secure enough in his eccentricities to take on the music business, even if from deep within the indie world. In 1999, with the release of the breakthrough album *I See a Darkness*, he lit on a new name, Bonnie 'Prince' Billy, and has mostly stuck with it ever since. The Oldham career is a guerrilla operation based on a big underground following, heavy rock-critic recognition, a film career – he was originally an actor and can be seen in John Sayles' *Matewan* (1987) – and a community of musicians who revere his work and who he records with, supports and, in his otherworldly words and ways, can be said to move among.

His previous two releases offer precious few clues to where Oldham has arrived at with *Lie Down in the Light*, in that each record he makes is a tack away from the one before. He is often in the studio, either working on his own material or making guest appearances that filter out on small labels. This, plus a constant touring schedule, has him plugged into the most hip recording scenes around. *The Letting Go* (2006) was recorded in Reykjavik, Iceland, with Björk's studio collaborator for the past ten years, Valgeir Sigurðsson. It is an austere, ghostly, string-driven folk album, with half-a-dozen good songs on it. *Ask Forgiveness* (2007) is a very sparsely instrumented eight-song EP, recorded in Philadelphia with Espers members Greg Weeks and Meg Baird. Except for one original number, the songs are an eclectic mix of covers, from Phil Ochs to Glenn

Danzig via Björk and the R&B star R Kelly. The record's packaging contains no list of song titles or musicians, and visual information is confined to seven full pages of photos of children from (at a guess) either Tibet or South America. The EP slipped out in Australia in the week before Christmas.

Given Oldham's recent wanderings and his reunion on this album with the engineer Mark Nevers in Nashville, *Lie Down* can be seen as a homecoming. It is also the best set of songs Oldham has had for some time. The inspiration is hard to discern: did the songs choose the studio, or did Nevers' studio and his approach help spawn the songs? The spark is there from the first guitar strums and the tickled, rich singing of the opening lines:

When there's just one thing I can do
You know I don't want to go through with it
When there's just one thing to get through
You know I don't want to go through with it

It's the Oldham philosophy distilled, right down to the song's title, 'Easy Does It', which encapsulates the sound and approach of the whole album. It's as if, with this record, Oldham has let go and – along with some fond self-contemplation – turned his mind to his family and his first loves in music, and made one of the sweetest and best records of his career.

The album has 12 songs, which for album unity is perhaps two too many. A pair of very strong numbers would bracket the record: 'Easy Does It' at the start, and the title track at song ten. Between them, Oldham weaves clusters of songs. 'You Remind Me of Something (Glory

Goes)', 'So Everyone', 'For Every Field There's a Mole' and '(Keep Eye On) Other's Gain' are philosophical musings in his stilted but still understandable style: "For every mole there's a hole with the soil that he stole and the sightlessness that lets him go free." A stretch of love songs follows, beginning with 'You Want That Picture', a clever turning on love and love-song clichés. Two poignant and perhaps autobiographical departure tracks are next, with the opening line of 'Missing One' – "I know that missing you has just begun" – setting the tone. A blazing rock song without drums breaks the spell. And then comes 'Lie Down in the Light', with its closing lines – "Time and again one of us falls behind / It's as if we tried to know what we can't really know" – seemingly a fitting place to end. Two further songs cloud the waters, going off to gospel and God.

The key to Will Oldham appreciation is working out what to take seriously and what is obscurantism and game playing. Judging him is always difficult. The songs across his career are generally good, and the instrumentation mostly interesting, but his artistic intentions can be hard to fathom. The game playing takes place on and off the records. For a start, there is the minimal, disorienting folk-art packaging, the lack of standard credits on the sleeves and the deliberately unattractive 'promotional' photos, one of which shows him down by a river in very thin underwear, belly protruding. Strangeness and knowing anti-show-business tactics are pushed to the fore. Meanwhile, his music can welcome, but it can also repel. His songs often have a sketchy, first-thrust feel to them, reinforced by the low-fi recording. But at heart he's a traditionalist: a Southern boy with an encyclopaedic knowledge of music who can sing frankly of sex in his life while still referencing 'the Lord'. Oldham intrigues even in his inconsistency, the crossed wires that distort the image of the serious singer–songwriter and how he appears to the world.

The sound of *Lie Down in the Light* is glorious folk-rock, which is not only easy on the ear but also serves to sugar-coat the unconventional lyrics. Oldham himself perfectly describes the sound in 'Easy Does It': "good earthly music". And how many great records fall into that category? The best of Neil Young, The Band, Fairport Convention, *American Beauty*-era Grateful Dead, and swathes of late-'60s to late-'70s country and folk. It's the warm steel-string acoustic guitars, the judicious use of pedal-steel guitar, deep bass, some fiddle, organ and piano, and voices – the lead vocal up high so every word is heard, and harmony vocalists cushioning the singer. On *Lie Down* it's Ashley Webber, a touch more country in her phrasing than other female vocalists Oldham has worked with recently, and Emmett Kelly, the guitar player with his classic high winsome harmonies. To get all this right and then down on tape, you need the right studio and a sympathetic engineer–producer. Mark Nevers, with his vintage-gear-filled suburban house, long a favourite with adventurous alt-country and rock musicians, offers just that. And the album, deep and laidback, is a joy to listen to.

The fascination with traditional music, be it country, folk or blues, is one of the strange tics of indie taste. The apparent simplicity and authenticity of the music is a reason for its appeal, as are the time-worn truths and mythmaking of the lyrics, which rock music obsessed with rebellion (no matter how dated) and adolescent sexuality seems to bypass. The sound of old recordings also attracts, whether it's the scratchy, dangerous blast of the '20s and '30s, the vitality of early rock and '50s blues, or the camp orchestration and earthy grooves of '60s and '70s country. Jeffrey Lee Pierce, with his band The Gun Club, picked up on this in the early '80s, and Jack White of The White Stripes is heir to Pierce's approach. When Will Oldham appeared, in the early '90s, this blending of indie and the traditional was well underway. Beck was in on it, and so too Uncle Tupelo, who morphed into Wilco and Son Volt while kick-starting the alt-country movement. This is Oldham's background, and the source of his melodies and his approach to song structure.

His strength is as a melodist. For someone with a confined vocal range and a guitar technique of no great virtuosity, Oldham manages to maintain a constant flow of quality songs. He has the knack of taking two or three chords and then spiralling the song out from a beginning you've heard before. He has great fun with melodic structures, letting strands and new ideas come into a song and then developing them convincingly to create something unique. He is not lazy, or happy to coast on roots-music clichés and become a John Prine wannabe. He is too dangerous for that, and his incorporation of rock music allows him to turn songs derived from folk or country rudiments into something weirder and thornier, without losing the power of the traditional sources. Examples abound on this album. 'Missing One', after an instrumental opening that never repeats, drops into a double verse and double chorus before going into a longish instrumental passage, followed by a verse with a new melody, then a repeat of the first verse, before an abrupt ending with a sung section of part of the long instrumental bit. Confusing and unconventional: yet it echoes the dysfunction and change suggested in the song's lyrics.

Lie Down in the Light is a charming, winning album by an artist whose work can be difficult to access. The lightness of the record is not to its detriment, and it joins *I See a Darkness* (1999) and *Ease On Down the Road* (2001) as high points in the Bonnie 'Prince' Billy catalogue. There are those who cling to their Dylan, Joni Mitchell, Springsteen and Van Morrison, bemoaning the lack of singer–songwriters possessing a seer's edge. These are different times, but Oldham is a contender. A place for some to start is perhaps Johnny Cash's spellbinding cover of Oldham's 'I See a Darkness' on the album *Solitary Man* (2000), produced by Rick Rubin. For those already au fait with Oldham's output, though, the news is that he's made yet another good record.

Confession & Hits (Hits & Confession)

Delta Goodrem's *Delta*

The first three album titles of Delta Goodrem's career provide a narrative of where she has come from and where she is now. *Innocent Eyes* to *Mistaken Identity* to *Delta*: the arc from birth to trial to arrival. It's a script she has written herself as she has progressed through a teenage pop career, a stint on *Neighbours*, success, scandal, Hodgkin's lymphoma, the split with her mother as manager, and a schedule that would have sunk any motivational speaker. *Delta* is her relaunch, a highly planned strategic operation that comes after she has got her life in order. And it's a public life, one led before the cameras and columns of a publicity-mad world. So we know she has a new man in her life, she lives in the UK with him and his two children, and the past years have been the first break in her career. *Delta* will tell us all of this, while at the same time attempting to make her an international superstar.

Delta Goodrem is a showbiz kid. She did her first television commercial at age seven; dancing, singing and piano lessons started soon after; and she had an artist-development contract with Sony at 15. At 19 came *Innocent Eyes* (2003). It's a good pop album, and just as importantly a strong showcase of her singing, songwriting and piano-playing talents. *Mistaken Identity* (2004) came too quickly. It's a much darker affair, presenting the muddle of a young life struck by stardom and strife. Track two is called 'The Analyst'. Track three, the album's title song, has the chorus, "The girl I used to be / Has a terrible case of mistaken identity / And yesterday's girl is not what you see." Which was true, but probably not what the record company wanted to hear. It sold well under half as much as her debut album, its chances further hobbled by a series of flat songs from Robbie Williams's songwriting partner, Guy Chambers.

Finding the right people to work with Goodrem has been a problem. There are the false starts to her recording career, the spread of producers on her first two albums, and the failed Guy Chambers experiment. It comes down to the strange package Delta Goodrem actually is. She is good-looking, but not in a pocket-sized, push-up bra kind of way. She can sing, but it's a powerful, 'hit them in the back row' voice. And she is a musician. So she's an oddity in the teenage-girl pop landscape. There is something old-fashioned and square about her, too, that must have the marketing people scratching their heads. What to do with her? Sexy? Windswept? Diva? Dance floor? *Delta*'s solution is to up the stakes on everything. If she is to crack the world market, presentation and sound have to be shiny and focused, with no identity crisis. Goodrem is ready, even if what gets lost along the way are some of the best things she has to offer.

A new beginning must be heralded. So the album starts with wafting synths and strings, lots of polished air and her vocal sounding like it has never sounded before, as if delivered from the heavens on wings. The opening line is a give-away, as well. Where before we had the gauche and obvious "A new beginning, a new chapter of my life", from *Mistaken Identity*'s first track, we now have Goodrem, when she does finally arrive, enigmatically muttering "Have you ever stared into the rain?" This is better. She has learnt metaphor, and overall the lyrics are more streamlined and considered, as if happiness and a few passing years have given her the power to say less and say it better. Not that the album is not totally self-obsessed and sprinkled with self-help one-liners. The first four songs throw up "I believe in miracles", "I was put here for a reason", "I don't crave what I have not" and most awkwardly of all, "I've been a soundboard tryin' to be neutral", which makes her sound like a mixing desk.

The principal revolution is in her sound. There is nothing on *Delta* that really has the feel of anyone playing in a room. This is state-of-the-art studio-crafted pop, built on beds of electronic textures, piano, touches of rock guitar and backing vocals so slick and soulless they may as well have been beamed down from Mars. Not that this is bad. It just marks it off from the sound of her other records which, although produced for the pop market, had a surprising amount of real instrumentation and grit to them. The producer list on *Delta* tells the story. This is the A-league: the guys that make Madonna, Backstreet Boys, Christina Aguilera and Sugababes records. Their instrument is the studio. Their aim is to top the pop charts in as many countries as possible, or in as many as carry MTV. Their sound is ultra-glossy and hook-heavy, and for Goodrem to have a shot at major stardom she had to take them on. But they come at a price.

Producers have always ruled the pop world, but there used to be just one of them on each record. Now there are five. There also used to be only one or two people writing each song; now there are four or five of them, too. The process began in the late '80s, when record companies realised that if they farmed out the production duties for a hit artist's record to as many producers as possible, each would try harder to make his or her track the lead single. So the company potentially had 12 hits on each album. *Delta* and almost all other pop-chart albums bear the consequences of this approach. Flow, experimentation and fun are gone. Desperation and an assault-like forcefulness have taken over, making the contemporary pop album an exhausting listening experience.

The number of songwriters grew when producers saw the money to be made in publishing and started writing songs themselves or demanding songwriting credits. The artists started to write their own lyrics both for artistic expression and because they saw the royalty cheques going to lyricists. And then there were the freelance songwriters. And this is how names started to bunch up at the end of song titles. On *Delta*, Goodrem's name is down on co-writing credits with three or more songwriters on ten of the album's 12 songs. Yet on *Innocent Eyes* she had two solo songwriting credits, and that album's smash single, 'Born to Try' – still the best thing she has ever done – she co-wrote with just one other person. A 'rejected' Goodrem-penned song for *Delta*, 'Writing Eyes on Me', has just been picked up and recorded by Celine Dion; given some of the tosh on this album, I wonder how bad it must be.

Despite these pressures of production and commerce, *Delta* does have a structure and a unity of purpose. The first four songs focus on her current situation and have a typically this-is-me-Delta feel to them. They are power-charged by the production, but each comes from a familiar place in the Goodrem style: the piano-tinkled intro winding its way to a knockout chorus. Song five is where the album changes, and the next five tracks seem to have been chosen to allow her to roam over genres for the first time in her career. There's a sense of testing the waters here, of seeing what else she is good at, while also providing the chance that something might bite in a different market. The best of them is 'You Will Only Break My Heart', which springs from the album with great joy. It's in the Kylie Minogue style, with an upbeat funky feel, and Goodrem eats it up. She drawls *babeee* like young female pop stars do, and it would make a challenging and potentially career-changing single.

Also in this group of five are the album's two outright stinkers, which Goodrem had no hand in writing. 'The Guardian' (no, it's not about the English newspaper) is a power ballad, and like most power ballads its masochistic take on love and its schlock music make it totally disheartening. 'Woman' is just plain ridiculous. I have problems with men that write songs called 'Woman', especially ones with such pleadingly cynical choruses as, "I'm a woman / A woman with a heart / And I need to be loved / 'Cause being just your woman is not enough." Goodrem tries her hardest, and songs such as these do suit her rallying vocal style, but the material has to be much better. She gets that again, thankfully, on the album's run-out. 'Brave Face', with its wonderful opening line – "Put your brave face on / The one you wore when you broke my heart" – returns to the biographical approach of the opening songs. 'One Day' has a Joy Division guitar line. And 'Angels in the Room', the big last love song, actually works as a big last love song because it's melodic, a little restrained and, like all of Goodrem's best work, truthful.

If there is one thing hampering the Goodrem modus operandi, it is the confines and rules of the musical world she works in. While it's true that her music is mainly aimed at girls aged between 8 and 15 (and the two girls I know in this bracket both bought her first album only), the style of the songs on *Delta*, with their quiet verses and sledgehammer choruses, nevertheless lends too much predictability to her music and to her. There is very little that is natural to this music, in the same way that there is nothing in *Delta*'s lyrics that touches on the outside world. Yet you feel she could write organic songs in and around the pop formula that would simultaneously allow her to grow and perhaps take an audience with her. Tellingly, she doesn't play piano on *Delta*. Not a note. The script of *Delta*, and where she is going, doesn't allow it – and that's fine. This is the big pop album a 23-year-old with her looks and voice has to make. And there may be more of them. But one day, she's going to have to break free of these kinds of songs and this kind of production, and drive herself with the piano and the songwriting talent she obviously has. And if her management was really thinking about the future, even with the cynical intent of just making her different from all the Britneys and Christinas and Gwen Stefanis of this world, they'd get her to do it sooner rather than later.

Setting Herself Apart

Sarah Blasko's *As Day Follows Night*

She's a restless soul, Sarah Blasko, three albums into her recording career: one made in Los Angeles, one in Auckland, and now her latest from Stockholm. Each has been shaped by its location. From LA came the neat, crafted pop of her debut, *The Overture & the Underscore* (2004); from Auckland there was the nautically themed swing and drama of *What the Sea Wants, the Sea Will Have* (2006); and in Stockholm – well, she recorded in the same studio as ABBA, the Swedish affinity for jazz is noticeable in the upright bass and percussion, and there is the talent of producer Björn Yttling, which is the obvious reason why Blasko was tromping through the snow in February and March this year. Yttling is both a member and producer of Peter, Björn and John, a Swedish pop band most famous for their left-field worldwide hit 'Young Folks' in 2006, a song that, besides featuring a whistling solo, impressed with its stripped-back mixture of groove and unusual natural instrumentation. The engagement of Yttling is another very smart move in a career built on astute and brave musical decisions.

At 32, the Sydney born and based Blasko finds herself in the enviable but also difficult position of sustaining a successful career in a shrinking album-sales market and a music scene that thrives on new faces and novelty. So far she has played it by instinct, with eye-catching album sleeves and clever videos, and generally conducting herself through the publicity and gimmick-driven maze of the music business with dignity and intelligence. As such she cuts a wilful and unusual figure, one who baffles those focused on the traditional short-term methods of career advancement, but her approach should ensure a long and satisfying career if she wishes to stay in music. Alongside the quality and seriousness of her work, and perhaps linked to its unorthodoxy, is the pleasure of her media presence, especially her interviews, which go against the normal line of shamefaced promotion and blind hope that dominates the pop-culture space. Blasko squirms under ARIA nominations and is willing to admit or ponder mistakes in print; it is an endearing trait, showing someone who is both honest and in constant self-reflection, qualities that abound in *As Day Follows Night* (2009).

The album is a triumph. It is one of those breakthrough records that only when it arrives and you hear the progression in spirit and song do you see the potential that was always there, just waiting for the artist to make the jump. And Blasko has made a leap. This is the best group of songs she has ever put together, her voice has never sounded so good, and her lyrics are divine. It's almost a shame that 'All I Want' doesn't start the album – the slower curtain-opener 'Down on Love' fulfils that role, as tentative mood songs have done on all her albums – because the first flush of all these developments is held in this great single. The initial realisation is that the veil has dropped: gone is the crimped, at times awkwardly compressed style of lyric-writing in favour of the elegant and enigmatic statement of the obvious. So "Between love we make divide, navigate / Confusion translates what you can't explain" from *The Overture & the Underscore* becomes "I don't want another lover / So don't keep holding out your hands / There's no room beside me / I'm not looking for romance". This is not to imply that the change has been sudden or unexpected. *What the Sea Wants, the Sea Will Have* was a transitional record, already showing a loosening of the lyrical knot and a preference for an adventurous sound driven by natural instrumentation; *As Day Follows Night* drives all the changes.

The first one may have come about while Blasko was writing the score for the Bell Shakespeare Company's production of *Hamlet* in 2008. An admitted confidence-building exercise for her songwriting, it also allowed her time to compose on the backstage piano between nightly vocal performances. It is tempting to draw further conclusions from her long exposure to Shakespeare's play. Is the dithering, self-absorbed hero an influence on the hand-wringing, does-he-or-doesn't-he-love-me central character of the album? Is "I'm finally mad, like a rush of blood to the head" in 'Lost & Defeated' a touch of Ophelia? And how far is Stockholm from Denmark, anyway? Nonetheless, for a songwriter preparing her first entirely self-composed set of songs for an all-important third album, Blasko has written a wonderfully melodic and diverse collection. Enter the producer Yttling, whom Blasko sought out, her admiration triggered as much perhaps by his production for the fine Scottish group Camera Obscura as by his work with his own band. Blasko and Yttling are a perfect match. He has fashioned a monster sound from the sparse ingredients of drums and bass and piano, building them big and full enough to carry many a verse and chorus with only Blasko's vocal on top. The production adds much to this album; outside of her singing and songs, it is the star – a thoughtful, delightful, sonic field of sparse instrumentation that has been expertly recorded.

The album's 12 songs tell a story. On *What the Sea Wants, the Sea Will Have*, nautical motifs, involving ships, storms, vessels, oceans and tides, were explicit in the lyrics and at times lacked some subtlety as metaphors for love and its troubles. On *As Day Follows Night*, the album's theme is far more skilfully embedded. Most of the songs revolve around a relationship involving three people. The narrator professes her love to a man who, it seems, can't leave another woman, despite her best efforts to cajole him to remain by her side. The woman is Night and the man is

Day, and the album's title alludes to their tangle. 'All I Want', with its magnificent stoicism, seems outside this circle of songs, but on every other number, from the opening track, 'Down on Love', where a case for happiness is put forward ("When all your life you've waited for someone to understand / To wake you up and speak your name"), to the demands of 'No Turning Back' ("I've put my heart right on the line / Now it's time my love, it's time"), to the dawning of truth in 'I Never Knew' ("But I never knew it would hurt like this / To let someone go against my wishes"), the dance of euphoria, disillusionment, pride and pain is charted. A resolution of sorts is found in 'Night & Day', the last song, where an early chorus of "Bitter night and a broken day" blooms in the record's final line to "Such a lovely night and a beautiful day". If it sounds overdone, it's not; the weave of night and day and all the meaning that can be drawn from these two words is strung very gracefully through the album's tracks.

But there is also a thrill-seeking giddiness to the album, as if to register that in the throes of uncertain love there are terrific highs to mix with the lows. Yttling's production helps out, pouncing on rhythms and always up for fun with weird instrument choices and melody lines. And Blasko goes with it too, stoking up songs such as 'We Won't Run' and 'Hold on My Heart' with big choruses that have a joy and a sense of abandonment that she has never achieved before. Leading the charge is her voice; recalling a sly 12-year-old one minute and Peggy Lee the next, it's high in the mix and as stripped of previous affectation as her lyrics. The mood is supported by the album's recording approach, which gives the vocal performances a first-take freshness that is backed by the live-in-the-studio feel of the musicianship. Songs don't fade but rather wind down naturally, often with a lyrical denouement at the finish. This could have been a much heavier album but instead it skids and skates, glockenspiels ring, percussion knocks and cracks, and Blasko, while not at peace, seems strong enough to dispense herself such cool and central wisdom as "Can't please somebody, can't please somebody else, until you've learnt to look after yourself".

Love has never been an easy game on any of Blasko's albums. There is real pain on *As Day Follows Night* and it is perhaps no coincidence that this is the first record of hers not to have the lyrics printed. Whether the kick to the heart was bigger this time, or whether she now has the power to transform it into greater art, is impossible to say. It has inspired a remarkable set of songs and, being the artist that she is – and great artists search and travel for a place to nail their feelings – she found a collaborator in Stockholm to help her make a wonderful record. A classic, in fact. Give her the ARIA now.

Modern Times and Times Before That

Bob Dylan's *Modern Times*

He's 65 years old now and he ain't slowin' down. Anyone thinking deep middle age was going to break Bob Dylan's stride and his will to impose himself as imperiously as possible on his times is mistaken. He set a frightening agenda in the '60s, and while things will never again be as giddy as that, just following the man these days is a full-time job. The situation is not helped by a perpetual raft of books and other assorted product that comes from the commentators. But it's Dylan himself, proving genius never dims, who is shooting sparks.

The last five years especially have seen him advance in a variety of unexpected fields: throwing his world view out to a million people through his weekly radio show, *Theme Time Radio Hour*, co-writing and starring in a film, *Masked and Anonymous* (2003), and writing a memoir, *Chronicles: Volume One* (2004), that astonished with its candour and wild poetic force. *Chronicles* ranks as one of Dylan's greatest triumphs, as revolutionary and evocative as his best album, the almighty *Blood on the Tracks*. Not bad for a man of 60-plus, doing about a hundred shows a year and still finding time to pen the odd tune.

The renaissance of Dylan as a recording artist began in 1997 with *Time out of Mind*. Before that there had been nearly two decades in the wilderness. There was a scattering of incendiary shows and good songs, but only one great album, *Oh Mercy* (1989). *Time out of Mind* brought us a new Dylan, or a new character Dylan felt conviction enough to play: the grizzled old man. Dylan has always needed a role to project his work into – Woody Guthrie acolyte, folk star, pop star, Nashville country gentleman, troubadour – and all of them elicit songs and a sense of mission from him. With his conversion to Christianity at the end of the

'70s he'd run to an identity as far from his early public self as possible, but it still produced a set of forceful songs. The '80s saw him touring with Tom Petty and The Grateful Dead. No role to play there, and no great album came.

"I ain't looking for anything in anyone's eyes," rasps a voice like that of an old gambler or sea captain. "My sense of humanity has gone down the drain," he says later. And then, "I'm just going down the road feeling bad, trying to get to heaven before they close the door." What brought Dylan to the new 'old' self of *Time out of Mind* one can only guess, but it gave him a voice – the bewildered survivor, wrecked and bemused, death at the door, women giving him trouble, a man in his mid-fifties ready to riff on this heavy load of new emotions. One ready to throw the Bible, the blues and anything else to hand at a world gone wrong and a career run off the tracks. It was magnificent. Here was a Dylan to luxuriate in again, fired up on despair and happy to wallow in every bad feeling he could find. He wrote a startling batch of songs, got Daniel Lanois in to produce it, and kick-started a momentum that runs to the present.

Better still is 'Things Have Changed', a song recorded for the soundtrack to *The Wonder Boys* (2000) that went on to win Dylan an Oscar. Here is the whole philosophy crunched into a moment. Over four verses, this minor-key blues shuffle offers up one hilarious line after another, as Dylan stacks it with out-the-side-of-the-mouth wisdom, absurd non sequiturs and anything wild that comes into his head. In so much of his best work, especially in the '60s and '70s, he had the ability to top one great line with another, then top it with another, a dazzling display of brilliance that left listeners and his songwriter contemporaries stunned.

He's at it again here:

I hurt easy, but I just don't show it
You can hurt someone and not even know it
The next sixty seconds could be like an eternity
Going to be low down, going to fly high
All the truth in the world adds up to one big lie
I'm in love with a woman who doesn't even appeal to me

The voice is dusty, close-miked; Dylan judges to the millisecond when to drop another bomb over the melody. The chorus is the payoff, an encapsulation of his post-'97 mood and a repudiation, right down to the obvious play on 'The Times They Are a-Changin'', of once-held ideals:

People are crazy and times are strange
I'm locked in tight I'm out of range
I used to care but things have changed

His next album, *Love and Theft*, came out on 11 September 2001. Lanois was gone as producer, replaced by Jack Frost – Dylan under a pseudonym. It's a strange record, a jumble of the brilliant, the bizarre and some treading of water, knocked into very little shape. The big surprise was a new turn in Dylan's songwriting: four jazz-chorded '30s pop songs. Their gentleness is blunted a little, however, by three of them being followed by howling blues numbers. Dylan is feisty throughout, clearly up and inspired after his last album, yet he's firing all over the place. The highlights jump out easily: the melodicism of 'Mississippi' and 'Sugar Baby', 'Lonesome Day Blues' and the mountain folk of 'High Water'. After *Time out of Mind*, it was a step down. The latest album, *Modern Times*, is a further step down again.

Actually, this is a tighter album than *Love and Theft*; ten songs to that album's dozen, and the roller-coaster turns through the genres are smoother. Jack Frost is again at the wheel and may not be the best servant to these songs; it would be interesting to hear Dylan with a producer again. His recording style is severe vérité: instruments are miked up, the band is rehearsed but never slick, Dylan sings live – press 'Record' and off we go. Which sounds great, a legend cutting loose in his later years and keeping it real, but Dylan needs more.

The songs need more, too, especially when Dylan calls upon a set of pre-rock 'n' roll influences, as he increasingly does. Lanois understood this; those old records had atmosphere and they had arrangements. Dylan is arrangement-shy and always has been. A typical Dylan-produced song, in the studio or on stage, consists of all the musicians starting together, playing together and finishing when Dylan gives them the nod. No one sits out. No one comes in just for a chorus. It's all pretty flat, and that's fine when the songs are top-notch and we listen to Bob sing. But as soon as they slip – as they surprisingly do on much of this album – you realise that someone else is needed to push Dylan on his material and the way it might sound.

The album starts with 'Thunder on the Mountain', and it's the weakest opening cut Dylan has put out for some time. Trouble is signalled in the second verse. A lyrical riff on soul star Alicia Keys feels lazy:

> *I was thinkin' about Alicia Keys*
> *Couldn't keep from crying*
> *When she was born in Hell's Kitchen*
> *I was living down the line*
> *I'm wondering where in the world Alicia Keys could be*

I been looking for her even through Tennessee

The tune is a 12-bar chug. None of the three other blues songs on the album is particularly inspired either. The blues is a cornerstone of Dylan's work, but he always needs an angle on it – some outrage, a big dose of humour – and when he doesn't have that he's talented enough to stay on cruise-control, using the form to meditate on and jab for meaning. The best here is 'Someday Baby', which distinguishes itself by being light and breezy. The others are too long and one of them, 'Rollin' and Tumblin'', is the blues standard of the same name, but with new lyrics.

The album really starts on track six, 'Workingman's Blues #2', which isn't a blues but rather a pretty piano-led melody, redolent of 'Forever Young', with Dylan stepping up and wheezing out, "There's an even haze settling over the town / Starlight at the edge of the creek". It's a song with a strong sentimental edge, Dylan gaining confidence verse by verse, and he reaches the midpoint with:

Now they worry and they hurry
And they fuss and they fret
They waste your night and days
Them I will forget
You I will remember always

Powerful stuff, and maybe the paucity of the songs before it accentuates its worth, but this is a big song all the way.

There are two others. 'Nettie Moore' and 'Ain't Talkin'' are reflections on or readjustments of songs that have gone before. In the little that Dylan has said about songwriting, he has made the point that originality can derive from just one change or twist to an existing song. Both these tracks have more than one twist. Both are relatively simple musical frames exploded by Dylan's lyrical finesse and singing, which is wired to the second. 'Ain't Talkin'' is clearer, possessing the more concrete setting of the two:

> *As I walked out tonight in the mystic garden*
> *The wounded flowers were dangling from the vines*
> *I was passing by yon cool and crystal fountains*
> *When someone hit me from behind*

It's a monster tale of revenge, misfortune, death, honour and gardening. Nothing you can put your finger on, of course; yet for atmosphere and grip, you just have to shake your head at the wonder of it all.

Time out of Mind, *Love and Theft* and *Modern Times* are seen by Dylan's record company and some critics as a trilogy, a term one can easily imagine eliciting a smirk and an eye-roll from Dylan. He has always been a grabber and swallower of influences, leading to treacherous turns between albums. But these last three recordings do have a unity to them, and it comes from the tightness of vision and the sense that Dylan is trying. His singing is always committed, not arch or parodic as it was in the '80s and often is when he's playing live. His songwriting is back, too – scattered and too reliant on roots, certainly, but he's written 15 really good songs over the last ten years. They bear comparison with the best of his '60s work, and more importantly they offer a new voice: cracked, lovelorn, pessimistic, gallows-humoured, still towering over his generation.

Old age suits him. It suits him the way being young did. It's a natural fit, for both are the traditional places where wisdom can flower: in the fired minds of the young and the dusty, wily utterances of the old. It's all the time in between that's the trouble. Dylan, though, survived all the crashes and the madness of his years, and survived well enough to leave himself fully stocked for a fruitful and significant late period. *Time out of Mind* remains the masterpiece; *Chronicles: Volume Two*, whenever that comes out, may be the next great thing he does. But he's putting three or four fantastic songs on each album, and smiling as the band runs through the ancient changes of the songs of his youth.

Turn Around: You Weren't Invited

The Yeah Yeah Yeahs' *Show Your Bones*

Karen O, Nick Zinner and Brian Chase are three good rock 'n' roll names; they're the Yeah Yeah Yeahs, another good rock 'n' roll name. They are from New York, and in this age of the fractured take on the classic rock line-up, they make up a vocals–guitar–drums combo. It's a hollow sound, giving each member room to scratch and howl their way around a downtown vision of garage rock. *Show Your Bones*, the Yeah Yeah Yeahs' second album, comes a full three years on from the successful debut *Fever to Tell*, a recording that they stridently declared they have no intention of repeating.

From the 2001 release of their first EP, the band looked interesting: jumping out of a crowded pack, it laid out five songs that highlighted the potential lines of attack. Two songs particularly impressed: 'Mystery Girl', an outrageously catchy swamp blues about a woman "grown men came to see" with a B-movie past ("They had found her under the sea / She said she came from cellblock three"), and 'Our Time', a song of a grandeur and style they haven't attempted since. Perhaps they got it too right the first time. It's a tower of a melody, built on Phil Spector lines and driven by Jesus and Mary Chain ooze. It became an anthem, with its hook-line "It's the year to be hated" working in reverse to thrust the band into the spotlight. They became famous quickly, and with Karen O's personal designer Christian Joy in tow and Spike Jonze doing the videos, they had some calling foul with that most dreaded (and often empty) of insults: hype.

For those high on the band's early recorded work, *Fever to Tell* was somewhat disappointing. In one of the most bizarre album sequencings ever, the three best songs were positioned last. The first eight appeared to be the band's clear-out of a backlog of spidery garage-rock numbers. There were some good tracks – 'Rich' and 'Date with the Night' – but as an opening salvo, it was strangely one-dimensional in light of the first EP. But 'Maps', the first of the album's final three songs, was something else altogether. The band's members have said, half jokingly, that they made *Fever to Tell* just to get this song down. 'Maps' is special; it's like a great early Pretenders single. Splintered, icy guitar lines from Zinner, and Karen O dropping the grunge and cooing "Oh say, say, say, wait, they don't love you like I love you": it's a tender, dreamy stretch of a pop song. The last two tracks, 'Y Control' and 'Modern Romance' (plus a hidden song), followed the lead of 'Maps', taking the gothic-garage sound, slowing it and shooting it into post-punk territory. The verdict: this was a group to watch, one that either didn't know its own strengths or was hip to the perversity of skewing expectations.

The band is a three-headed monster. Karen O is the attention-grabber. With her asymmetrical haircut and early-'80s trash-girl couture, she immediately inspired imitators on the street and on the stage. Her vocal style is a high yelp; as a performer and media creature she is totally engaging. Brian Chase, the drummer, is percussive and tight, playing straight when needed, flaying when drama is called for. He's jazzy, and reminiscent in spirit and invention of that other great drummer without a bass player, John Densmore of The Doors. Nick Zinner may just be the star of the three. This boy can play guitar. He sticks rigidly to the song and he's a sonic architect. He can do swoop-down like Rowland S. Howard in Birthday Party mode. He can do early Cure/Siouxsie and the Banshees creepy jangle, and then blow it up stadium-size, like Billy Corgan. Rockabilly, rock, post-punk and eerie campfire strum are all in his repertoire. He's already guesting on other artists' tours and, to cap it off, he's just published the almost obligatory I-have-arrived-as-a-rock-star set of photographs, *I Hope You Are All Happy Now*.

Changes are afoot on *Show Your Bones*, and they are rung in immediately. Tight acoustic strumming brings in the single 'Gold Lion'. It's pop, and it immediately jolts each band member into focus. Karen O's voice is rich; the drums have lost the live-in-a-warehouse clang and are sitting more conventionally in the mix; Zinner's excellent guitar work wraps up the package. With the acoustic-tinged 'Way Out' next, it's a crisp beginning. It has one checking the album credits for the recording location (Brooklyn), for the feel here is Beck's California. This rustic approach emerges full-blown towards the end of the album in 'The Sweets' and 'Warrior', both of which start with desolate acoustic strokes before flaring out with heavy electric guitar. You could call it dark folk.

It's an odd album, and one that appeals far less than it should. All the vital ingredients seem to be in place: a three-year lay-off, a willingness to expand, a sense of adventure from a band that knows the workings of song construction. Perhaps it's the wish to annihilate the past so absolutely that has led the group too far from what it does best. A minor identity crisis is posted in the sequencing: the album really begins on track five with 'Honeybear', which is the first in a smooth and logical run of songs that don't seem forced in their ordering. The first four songs have agenda written all over them, robbing the whole album of a satisfying arc. After the opening two pop songs come the two heaviest cuts on the record, 'Fancy' and 'Phenomena', and they're nasty pieces of work. Here, their earlier spiky art-rock takes on a more classic shape. Heart and Led Zeppelin are evoked in style, wattage and song trajectory – especially in 'Phenomena', which employs the Page–Plant trick of a slamming chorus followed by dream sequences and washes before crashing back hard on the chorus riff. But it's questionable whether the rock spirit of the Yeah Yeah Yeahs is best channelled into crunching cock rock.

The finest numbers are those close in style to the band's earlier work. 'Honeybear' leaps with exuberance. It's as if the shackles have been kicked off and the group has relaxed into artful abandonment. "Turn around, you weren't invited," the song's opening line, works as an ironic invitation to the album proper. (Until then, due to Karen O's vocals being buried in the mix and her typically New York non-linear mash of lyrics, the only clear words on the album are in the choruses of the first four songs.) 'Mysteries' is magnificent, going at 200 miles an hour, with Karen O deploying her best lyric-trick of sliding in and out of a situation, giving just enough information to draw an emotional response amidst the whirlwind. The last song, 'Turn Into', does it as well. Like 'Mysteries', it seems to wind up and then explode with gorgeous melody, the band members galloping as one yet each still trying to be the first across the line.

The pop openers 'Gold Lion' and 'Way Out' show a path forward. The rock songs that follow don't, but it's still a genre that the group could master or mutate. This is a band of three very talented individuals; they may quickly make a better album than *Show Your Bones*. But until then the Yeah Yeah Yeahs will remain one of those unusual bands with a few killer songs on each record. The rest of the tracks, while not making you wonder how they came up with the good ones in the first place, leave you rather cold. That unpredictability will keep me listening to them. I suppose I could wait for the greatest hits but, knowing the Yeah Yeah Yeahs, they won't put any of them on it.

To the Heart

Geoffrey Gurrumul Yunupingu's *Rrakala*

Elcho Island is 560 kilometres from Darwin, off the northeast Arnhem Land coast. A strong musical community there has produced members of Yothu Yindi, the lead singer of the Warumpi Band, George Burarrwanga, the country/gospel band Soft Sands, the Chooky Dancers and Geoffrey Gurrumul Yunupingu. Gurrumul was born blind in 1970. He learnt to play a right-handed guitar left-handed and is proficient on a number of other instruments, including keyboards and drums. For some years he was a member, with some of his cousins, of Yothu Yindi, which, besides extending his musical experience, would have given him an introduction to the music business and touring. After leaving Yothu Yindi he formed the Saltwater Band in 1996, the same year he played one of his songs, 'Djarimirri', to Michael Hohnen, a fresh-faced Melbourne bassist who had come to Elcho Island to conduct a music course. Deeply impressed, Hohnen took ten years to coax Gurrumul to begin work on a solo album of his songs, played primarily to the stripped-back accompaniment of acoustic guitar and Hohnen's upright bass. *Gurrumul* was released in 2008 on Skinnyfish Music, with expected sales optimistically set at 20,000 copies; 140,000 copies in Australia later – with ARIA awards, worldwide world music chart success, gushing high-level international press and a performance with Sting doing 'Every Breath You Take' on French TV in between – comes *Rrakala*.

On first exposure, *Gurrumul* draws forth a comparison with another recent breakout artist with a stand-alone voice and a compelling cycle of songs: Antony, of Antony and the Johnsons, and their *I am a Bird Now*. It may seem a strange coupling – Indigenous, remote island man and transgender, New York underground art singer – but both men offer up songs sung in angelic voices that chronicle, in surprisingly similar ways, an intuitive, highly sensitive response to their surroundings. Both men seek redemption in nature: Gurrumul, singing mostly in the Yolngu language, mixes landscape, animal life and family into a spiritual reverie;

Antony's mythology sees nature and the feminisation of society as the only means of human survival. In both cases the result is an otherworldly record that seems instantly to exist on no other terms but its own. And so it was in the marketplace, where a honey-voiced Indigenous singer–songwriter eschewing direct political and social commentary broke through on word-of-mouth recommendation and stellar reviews.

Seen in relation to *Rrakala*, *Gurrumul* now seems a more traditional and straightforward singer–songwriter album. Here perhaps is the cream of the material from a long apprenticeship that ended in mastery of the songwriter's craft. They are stirring songs, highly melodic and heart wrenching, accompanied by the singer's own fingerpicked steel guitar. Hohnen's bass is artful and supportive, at times more 'felt' than heard in the mix. Some electric guitar is often the only colouring added to a spartan recording plan that in essence says, "Here are 12 fantastic songs – enjoy." And, in fact, little was needed in the way of instrumental flavour because the singing takes up so much room. Bruce Elder, the longstanding folk and roots music critic for the *Sydney Morning Herald*, called it "the greatest voice this continent has ever recorded". It may be, but it is also more than a voice; it is 'voices' and the way they are employed that could in the end turn out to be a greater achievement than the voice itself. Often songs begin with Gurrumul singing in a bass-toned natural register; quickly a high harmony enters to offer melting sweetness and contrast, and then can come block-layered harmonies; add humming, scat sung noises and clicks to this, and the most intriguing and revolutionary aspect of the man's art is the way he uses his voice.

In between the two solo albums came *Malk*, the third Saltwater Band album, and on it were three songs from *Gurrumul*, re-recorded. The Saltwater Band, also produced by Hohnen, play a ska/reggae-fied version of world music pop and their versions suggest the unpredictable pros and cons of electrifying a folk song. 'Galiku' and 'Baywara' are both quicker in tempo than the originals. The former benefits from – or at least can accommodate – the added instrumentation and swing, while the latter, with its heartbreaking opening line, 'I heard my mother from the long distance making me cry', loses a lot of intimacy and power in the new arrangement. *Rrakala* doesn't follow any of the roads opened up by the Saltwater Band. Instead it is a companion to *Gurrumul*: another 12-song set, with clean, minimal production and Gurrumul's singing at the centre. Yet for all the surface similarities, the differences between the two solo albums are deep: the grand uplifting melodies are fewer and the mood is sadder, while musically the new album is more adventurous, side two especially, which with its spare sounds and cyclical melodies tends to a style bordering on art music.

Like its predecessor, *Rrakala* opens with the album's most instantly attractive melody, in this case 'Gopuru'. 'Mala Rrakala' continues the mood, but where *Gurrumul* soared off at this point with 'Bapa' and 'Gurrumul History (I Was Born Blind)', *Rrakala* starts a meditative journey, surfacing for the delightfully clipped 'Ya Yawirriny', and followed, with the entry of Gurrumul on piano for 'Warwu', by a five-song run that barely moves above ballad tempo. The trance-like atmosphere of this group of songs, and of Gurrumul's music in general, comes from the melodic structures of his songs. Absent is the tight formula of much western pop, with its quick interlocking verses and choruses, and often a third 'middle eight' section introduced after the second chorus. Instead Gurrumul either writes one highly melodic chord sequence, tweaking it with his arrangement, or two or three such sections or blocks, and ingeniously shuffles them in and out of each other. The mood is always stately and deliberate; this music has its roots in the melodic end of folk, with its switching of major and minor chords, aided by touches of soul, gospel and, as Paul Kelly noted in the recent February issue of *The Monthly*, a '*fado* style', heightened on *Rrakala* by flourishes from Gurrumul's nylon-string guitar.

He's a very talented musician. And it's remarkable that while the singing and songs impress, the expert acoustic-guitar licks, the James Burton–style electric-guitar picking, the piano and the brushed drums are also all his work. It's rare, too, for a singer–songwriter to be able to score their own music and personalise it to the extent that Gurrumul can. To go with the expansion of instrumentation on the new album there has been a shift in recording location from Melbourne's Audrey Studios to Avatar Studios (formerly the Power Station) in New York. *Gurrumul* was beautifully recorded, but Avatar has imparted an added presence and spaciousness – and among the beneficiaries is the upright bass, which is now on its own and able to be appreciated as it links up and supports the guitar and voice. If the decision to record there is that of the album's producer, Michael Hohnen, then it is one more bold and good decision to come from him. Gurrumul is the discovery, but in his shadow is the emergence of Hohnen as a first-class record producer. There'd be a lot of big studio names who would swamp these songs, or, despite realising restraint was required, still add too much. Each overdub from Hohnen seems considered, and every temptation resisted only makes these songs sound bigger.

"Gu nilimurru nhina yarrarra'yun" is a lyric line from 'Warwu' and an example of the 'look' of the Yolngu language. Sung by Gurrumul with rolled 'r's and a clipped tongue, the melodies at times evoke the drama of the Mediterranean folk song; there is even a sense when listening to him of hearing someone singing in Portuguese or Italian. A language loved and caressed in song can often be appreciated by non-speakers. That's the power of Gurrumul. Yes, his songs are a mantra of home, family, ancestors, sunsets, mourning and crying – that's what it says in the English translations of his lyrics. But through his art and the care he takes, he's able to skip the 'translation' stage and go where only great musicians can go – straight to the heart.

Lost Women Found

The discovery of Vashti Bunyan, Sibylle Baier & 'Connie' Converse

"When did you write that? How did you happen … to … uh …" The nervous and incredulous male voice stops there on the tape. It's 1954 and Connie Converse, the singer and songwriter who has elicited this response, has just recorded one of her songs onto the reel-to-reel. Fifty-five years later the quality of the song is undeniable and the questions put to her still have a strange poignancy. How did she write these songs? How did it happen that at the great cultural crossroads of post-war New York there was a lone woman writing songs on guitar with a sophistication of lyric and melody unmatched by any other folk songwriter of the time? It stumped the man who was recording her, and her answers, if she gave any, aren't on the tape.

How she went unnoticed in her day is easier to explain. She had no manager or agent with uptown show-business connections, and she didn't perform in public. All she had were the songs and her circle of friends. But it has turned out to be enough, as it did for fellow singer–songwriters Sibylle Baier and Vashti Bunyan, all of whom put songs in a bottle and kissed them goodbye, not knowing that one day the bottle would drift back, carrying the dreams and emotions of youth, to be picked up by an audience far larger and more appreciative than the one that greeted the music at its inception.

Vashti Bunyan was supposed to be the new Marianne Faithfull. She had the beauty, the ethereal, wispy voice, and she had a ballad written by Jagger and Richards. All of which had been enough for Faithfull to have a hit with 'As Tears Go By', but Vashti's first single, 'Some Things Just Stick in Your Mind', bombed. She was 20 and it was 1965. Unlike Faithfull, Vashti was a songwriter, a purveyor of fine melancholic acoustic folk more akin to the continental pop of French star Françoise Hardy. There were more singles over the next few years, written by Vashti, but they also failed to chart.

By '68 she'd had enough and set off on an adventure typical of the time. The goal was a commune on the Isle of Skye being set up by the pop singer Donovan, a friend of Vashti's travelling and romantic partner, Robert Lewis. The twist was that they set off from London up the A6 in a horse-drawn wagon, finally arriving two summers and a winter later to find Donovan and the commune gone. Along the way, she had written a suite of songs that documented the dreams and scenes that were pointing the travellers to a new way of life. These songs became the candlelit core of Vashti Bunyan's first album, *Just Another Diamond Day*, released in 1970.

The record was produced by her supporter and fan Joe Boyd, for the wonderfully named Witchseason Productions. The musicians were from Fairport Convention and The Incredible String Band, with string and recorder arrangements by Robert Kirby, famous now for his work with Nick Drake. Yet the album received that most dispiriting of responses: indifference mixed with the sting of critical hostility. Vashti, taking this as both professional and personal failure, quit the music business and turned to the raising of her three children, the tending of her animals and the graft of self-sufficiency in farms and communities ranging from the Isle of Berneray in the Outer Hebrides to rural Ireland. During these 20 years of hard back-to-the-land living, she wrote no songs and made no music, shelving her music career and the perceived artistic and commercial disaster of *Diamond Day* to the extent that her children, upon finding a copy of the album in her possession, could only listen to it in secret in the family car. It was the attainment of adulthood of her elder son and daughter that drew her back into the urban world of Edinburgh in the late '90s, and it was sheer curiosity a few years later that made her type her name into an internet search engine. She found that *Just Another Diamond Day* was going for $2000 a copy.

Not every album released and sold in small quantities in the early '70s commands such prices. The producer and the musicians, and their connections to what is now regarded as a golden era of experimental folk music, would have helped, but the magic lies in the record itself. It's a beautiful album, as otherworldly as you'd expect, with all the dew-dropped atmosphere of late-'60s counter-cultural folk.

There are the fifing whistles, recorders, banjos and strings, but what serves the album best is its gorgeous songs. The melodies have pop craft that lifts them above the usual three-chord strum, and the lyrics eschew rose-tinted hippy glasses or the dodge of medieval mysticism for something softer and more real: the wonder of nature in the landscape, the appreciation of its beauty lost in the rush of modern life. The album is a glimpse of another world, and the trumpeting of the recorders and whistles makes that call all the more noble and magnificent. At the front is Vashti, her rallying call a soft prayer to the rainbow rivers, to the windows over the bay, the glow-worms lighting the way to a place where "fairy stories are whispered till they're real".

When reissued in 2000, the album received the rapturous reviews it had deserved the first time around. Also waiting were the young hippies and hipsters of the gathering freak-folk movement led by Devendra Banhart, who had *Just Another Diamond Day* pegged as essential listening and the story of the horse and wagon down as myth. Vashti triumphantly toured and in 2005, 35 years after the release of her debut album, came the follow-up, the strong and sombre *Lookaftering*. A lyric from the album's best song, 'Wayward', tells the whole story:

I wanted to be the one
With road dust on my boots
And a single silver earring
And a suitcase full of notes

And a band of wayward children
With their fathers left behind
All in their castles in their air
And houses in their land

She is currently somewhere on the American West Coast with the young folk-rockers Vetiver, making album number three.

In Stuttgart in 1970 there was a group of bohemian young Germans who were interested in film, music, art and politics. One of them was the future filmmaker Wim Wenders; another was an actress, artist and future songwriter called Sibylle Baier. In 1973 she appeared in Wenders' *Alice in the Cities*, and by then she had recorded a collection of her own songs, sung in English and backed by her acoustic guitar, on a reel-to-reel machine in her living room. She gave Wenders, and probably other friends too, a cassette copy. And that's the end of the story, except that 35 years later Wenders, while standing in front of Reckless Records in Chicago, sees a familiar face, a young face, on a record cover in the shop window. It's Sibylle Baier. He rushes into the shop to buy a copy of the music he's been carrying around on a battered cassette since the '70s.

Colour Green came about through Baier's first son, Robby, who grew up with his mother in the United States to become a musician and record producer. He compiled a CD of her unreleased songs and gave a copy to J Mascis from Dinosaur Jr, who forwarded them to the Orange Twin label, which released the album to insider acclaim. Wim Wenders, reacquainted with Baier's music and still in contact with her, immediately commissioned her to write a new song for his film *Palermo Shooting*. She did: it's called 'Let Us Know', and for some, hearing this song was the door back to *Colour Green* and the life of Sibylle Baier.

The album is totally intriguing: an artefact that offers the pleasures of its songs and the mysteries of the tomb. The music is similar in style to that of Leonard Cohen and Joni Mitchell. But here's the scary bit – it's also as good. It is doing *Colour Green* a disservice to linger on comparisons, but from Cohen there is the plucked jauntiness of the nylon-string melodies and the European dance of melancholy and poetry; from Mitchell there's the advanced guitar technique and a jazzy coolness in the singing. From both comes the idea of the song as confessional. That's the frame, but what Baier does with it is truly amazing. Here are 14 songs that many an artist would be happy to sprinkle over a four-album career. Running concurrent with the vast pleasures that the record gives are the questions it throws up. How does a young German woman learn to sing and write in English so well? Where did the remarkable guitar playing come from? Where was the folk scene (in Stuttgart?) that would have nurtured and supported her? Answers aren't forthcoming from the reclusive Baier, and because she had no standard 'rock' career there are no interviews to go back to. Instead there is an enigma, a new great singer–songwriter popping out of the air, her existence only known to us because her son gave a CD of her songs to the lead singer of Dinosaur Jr.

If Vashti Bunyan and Sibylle Baier are big stories, with their fragile and treasured songs like golden eggs lost and finally found, then the tale of Connie Converse is something else altogether, a drama so sprawling, with a denouement so unexpected, that Hollywood can only gaze in wonder: Reese Witherspoon or Kate Winslet is probably practising the acoustic guitar right now.

Elizabeth Eaton 'Connie' Converse was born in Laconia, New Hampshire in 1924 to strict God-fearing parents. Exceptional at school, she gained an academic scholarship to Mount Holyoke College and had one kind of life in order and on track when she threw it in and left, after two years' study, for New York City. In 1949 she bought a guitar and soon after started writing songs. She worked as a printer and lived alone in Greenwich Village. A man-about-town with an ear for music by the name of Bill Bernal heard her in private gatherings in Manhattan and alerted his amateur recording friend Gene Deitch. It is his incredulous voice that can be heard on the tape asking "when" and "how" at the end of one of her songs.

There were a few sessions at Deitch's house, with most of the recordings done by 1954. There were no commercial recordings made and Converse's approaches to publishing houses with her songs were met with rejection. In 1961, with no breakthrough in her music career, she left New York for Ann Arbor, Michigan. Through her brother, who was a professor at the University of Michigan, she got a secretarial job and soon after became editor of the university's *Journal for Conflict Resolution*. By 1973, heavy drinking was fuelling her depression, and colleagues and friends pooled money for her to spend six months in England. The following year, back in the US, she wrote a series of goodbye notes to those around her, drove off in her Volkswagen bug and was never heard of again.

Gene Deitch went to Prague in 1959, where he has lived and worked ever since. (In 1961 his short animated film *Munro*, written by Jules Feiffer, won an Academy Award.) In 2004, at the age of 80, he was invited back to New York City by the music historian David Garland to appear on his renowned and long-running radio show *Spinning on Air*. Deitch brought along some of his old live recordings to play, slipping in a song called 'One by One' by Connie Converse; after 50 years she was getting her first airplay. Garland was immediately impressed and interested in her story, as were two listeners, Dan Dzuda and David Herman, who began the slow process of compiling a Connie Converse album. There were two sources for the tapes: Deitch's collection in Prague, and a filing cabinet in Ann Arbor containing recordings Connie sent back to her ever-supportive brother during the early 1950s. In March 2009, *How Sad, How Lovely*, containing 17 original songs by Connie Converse, hit the market.

It is both a historical document and a living, breathing album by a musician whom Garland describes as possibly the first American singer–songwriter. If nothing else, the record challenges history. The question is whether to see her as a wild precursor to the singer–songwriter movement that began in the early '60s, or as a singular artist, an Emily Dickinson figure, caught out of time, working enclosed and unknown. There were folk-based singer–songwriters in the '50s, such as Pete and Peggy Seeger and Malvina Reynolds, writer of 'Little Boxes' and 'Morningtown Ride' (later covered by The Seekers). But these were primarily political writers, and none foresaw the coming wave of youngsters who would drag poetry and private feelings together to the accompaniment of an acoustic guitar. Connie Converse was doing this, alone and unaided, making a deep and marvellous connection between lyric and song that allows us to enter the world of an extraordinary woman living in mid-twentieth-century New York.

They are a most peculiar bunch of songs. Part of this is due to Converse's cultural isolation, and part to the songs' connection to a period of popular culture that is now more than 50 years in the past. It is found in the prim and precise vocal style, and the crisp, concise strut and Broadway and popular-song shadings of her guitar playing. As strange as it is to hear folk music without the '60s inflections – the flatness of the rhythm, the slurred singing, the influence of the blues – equally strange is hearing early '50s music with post-'60s emotional honesty. The most striking songs on the album, 'One by One', 'There Is a Vine' and 'Honeybee', portray a woman often waiting, lonely, proud, difficult and in need of attention or affection. Women weren't writing these kinds of songs in the 1950s; they weren't writing songs so desperate or pure of feeling, or so flippant and wild. It is hard to imagine anyone else from the era packing this moral ambiguity into a song:

People say a roving woman is likely not to be
Better than she ought to be
So when I stray away from where I've got to be
Someone always takes me home

Or the wit and spark of "Up that tree there's sort of a squirrel thing / Sounds just like we did when we were quarrelling". Family and friends regarded Converse as smart, possessing an intelligence that Deitch recalls as intimidating, and it's all through these songs. Yet there are no real relationships in the narratives, no recognisable congress between men and women, only 'The Man in the Sky', the sailor boyfriends happier at sea in 'Father Neptune', and in 'Johnny's Brother', the brother of the man you marry who may be the father of your child.

One last thought: it's amazing how uncompromising the music of these three women is. Connie Converse and Sibylle Baier had nothing to lose: they were amateurs in front of a tape machine. Vashti had a career. But the songs they wrote don't shirk. This is confrontational music that's soft, melodic and tender, and the truths these women are putting over have a power that many an artist screaming and growling over noise would be afraid to go near. So ultimately it's brave; brave to have done it in the first place and braver still to go on, knowing that the songs probably weren't ever going to reach the audience they so richly deserved. Sibylle Baier gave out cassettes, Vashti Bunyan tried and withdrew, and Connie Converse left the copyrights of her songs to her brother in the face of 20 years' indifference to her music. She knew.

Embers Re-Flamed

Meg Baird's *Dear Companion*

In the tangled undergrowth of the indie-rock scene there are certain musical genres that re-emerge with some regularity. New wave, no wave, country, disco and garage rock all have their time in the sun, and then come back later in a new mutation. But three or four years ago, a genre appeared on the scene that hadn't really made its presence felt before: psychedelic folk.

The originators of this music came from a gnarled branch of the British music world of the mid-to-late '60s. The commercial face was Donovan; behind him and deeper underground were The Incredible String Band, Fairport Convention, Tyrannosaurus Rex and a host of other bands and individuals putting traditional folk sounds into the fire of the changing times. It was potent music wedded to the notion of hippie, and it died somewhere in the early '70s, when the glad rags and incense hit the unforgiving light of the new decade. With it went the far-out and far-reaching sense of journey – locked away, heard in the odd singer–songwriter, its traces found at the edges of every psychedelic-rock revival – but the full blast has not come back until now.

Its return is marked by certain changes. Drug use seems to be down, the major record labels are at arms-length and the starry-eyed acid-for-the-first-time lyrics are gone. The latter is the key change in a movement that now goes under a variety of names, including 'freak folk' and 'free folk'. For while the predominantly acoustic nature of the music remains intact, with all its flights and open-tuned explorations, the vision is more grounded, hooked on nature and ecology, slippery relationships and the kooky take on life that you find in outsiders (especially young Americans) writing their first songs.

The avatars with breakthrough albums were Joanna Newsom and Devendra Banhart; it was they who tipped off the underground that something was happening. Newsom is the harp-playing, high-voiced songstress and Banhart the Nick Drake-loving mystic who looks like he's just walked off the set of a peyote-fuelled Western. Both had hippie parents and both were exposed to very good record collections at a young age. This is something common to many of these new folk artists: a hunger to dig for music not only outside the mainstream but outside the usual slipstreams of indie taste. So interviews are filled with reverent references to long-forgotten or long-out-of-fashion artists who provide inspiration. The list swings from cult singer–songwriters and acoustic blues players (Michael Hurley, Mississippi John Hurt, Karen Dalton), to Brazilian and Eastern music, to the hippie end of Californian rock and folk (Caetano Veloso, Grateful Dead, Linda Perhacs), and they give as good a description as any of the music the new generation makes.

Two important groups have crawled out of the mass: Vetiver and Espers. Vetiver are from San Francisco, and they're an ever-expanding collective built around the guitar playing and songs of Andy Cabic. They have put out two albums, *To Find Me Gone* (2006) being the latest. Good songwriting and an acute sense of atmosphere are to the fore; the albums are rambling and acoustic, with a delightful early-'70s vibe that doesn't drown in its influences. Espers hail from Philadelphia, and are a different beast altogether. They're a six-piece, and their second album, *Espers II*, shows them moving away from the acoustic approach of their first disc to something far more textured and electric. There are now soft drums behind a sound that goes to the outer stratospheres of space rock, while still sounding like it's linked to the seventeenth century of dying maidens and moon cycles. This gorgeous seven-track album, which I first heard months after its release, was my favourite album of last year.

If *Espers II*, with its eight lines of gear listed in the album credits, is the dark river, then Meg Baird's *Dear Companion* is the brook. She is a member of Espers, and her solo album is a bare counterpoint to the layered and progressive tendencies of the band's LP. Recorded in warm tones by fellow Esper and engineer Greg Weeks, Baird sings the ten songs accompanied only by her guitar. No arrangements or producer intent – this is someone singing songs into a microphone in an attic, and it's great.

Of course, there's all manner of art and decision implicit in the approach. First of all, Weeks has recorded her well. The guitar is woody and full, and Baird's voice is likewise. Why isn't this done more often? And why, especially in Australia, can't engineers pull off something like this without it sounding thin and tinny? Baird's choice of material is masterful, too. It's a fine mix of traditionals, such as 'The Cruelty of Barbary Allen' and 'Willie O' Winsbury'; intriguing covers, including 'Do What You Gotta Do' by Jimmy Webb and 'All I Ever Wanted' by New Riders of the Purple Sage; and two strong songs of her own. The sequencing of the record is a great weave, with the longer narrative ballads followed by the shorter, sweeter 'pop' songs, and with the help of a little double-tracking of Baird's voice by Weeks, the album never falls from your attention.

What Baird and Espers and Vetiver are doing is brave. There is a lifestyle aspect to this as well; it's not just the music from the late '60s that is being re-awoken, but also that era's beliefs and outlook on life. The communal aspects and the soft-eyed gaze at the wonder of the world have filtered through, and it's perhaps no coincidence that a lot of this music, with its emphasis on withdrawal and the past, is coming out during the second term of the Bush presidency, and when the planet is in peril. The kids are in the woods.

It's brave also in the face of a music business geared to the quick shot and the relentless manufacture of the 'new'. The music of these English-folk-loving groups fits the times. Other kindred spirits are around – Will Oldham, M Ward, Jolie Holland – but lately it's been the Vetiver–Espers–Baird contingent, and the deep trip they are taking in reviving and expanding a curious corner of rock history, that grabs. It's almost a case of unfinished business, the dying embers re-flamed, and *Dear Companion* is a vital part of the campaign.

Nihilistic Ear-worms

Franz Ferdinand's *You Could Have It So Much Better*

If this album review was a Franz Ferdinand song it would almost be over by now. These boys don't hang about. Short, sharp songs, guitar riffs bouncing all over the place, storming choruses, a deft cultural reference or two and then they're off, down the road, laughing in their tight, coloured clothing, thinking we've done it again. Another ball of guitar hooks, another broken-plated song – glued back together our way.

Franz Ferdinand don't just come from any music town. They're from Glasgow, a place steeped in indie-rock legend. Orange Juice. Aztec Camera. The Jesus and Mary Chain. Teenage Fanclub. Belle and Sebastian. Every four or five years this city has managed to produce a major rock band. It's a scene keen on its own history, a town that loves pop, country, black music (old and new) and anything even vaguely camp or obscure.

The Strokes' rock revolution of 2001 was starting to get very boring. Identikit bands were popping up all over the place and locking into the formula: rock-and-roll pop songs cut clean, new-wave intentions, late-'70s street fashion and a fixation with New York as the new–old underground rock capital. Franz Ferdinand landed in early 2004, adding a much-needed dose of cut and suave. They were art-school boys, not pretend ones but the real thing from Glasgow, who lived and played in a place called The Chateau, who named themselves after an assassinated Austrian archduke, who mixed post-punk Scottish nous with an eclectic combing of '80s influences. They seemed new and exciting. More importantly, they had songs, the best bunch of cleanskinned rock and pop songs since The Strokes' first album.

The founder, songwriter, lead singer, and one of two guitarists in the band is Alex Kapranos. He'd been floating round the edges of the Glasgow scene for at least ten years until he finally facilitated rock's magic combination: great rock songs and the right people to play them. Once he had that, they were off. Their self-titled debut record won every album-of-the-year award going, and has set the fashion and musical agenda ever since. Their coda, their greeting card to a wall of waiting journalists, was: "We're making music for girls to dance to." They brought back the spectre of slinky sex and the disco, missing in indie-rock land since the very early '80s when the great forebears of all things wonderful, Orange Juice, were talking about combining Chic and The Velvet Underground, and when New York's Ze Records was trying to marry art and the dance floor.

Given all this – their small record label, their art-school approach, Glasgow – Franz Ferdinand were expected to sell no more than 10,000 records. They had something else up their sleeve, though. They could write rock songs. For all the newness that they promised and promoted in image and interview, they had a link to The Strokes and other big-selling bands. Rock riffs get you out of the ghetto. Rock riffs fill concert halls and reach row 150 at the rock festival. The Germans call it *Ohrwurm*, or ear-worms – big, compulsive, brain-lodging riffs – and these lodged not in 10,000 brains but in millions.

You Could Have It So Much Better arrives only 18 months after *Franz Ferdinand*. This is a smart move, deflating the expectation and pressure that can cripple a band working on the follow-up to a successful first album. It also gives the impression of a band on the move and not afraid to play its second card. It's a much rockier record, with tougher production. It doesn't draw breath until song seven when the first ballad comes in, the very pretty 'Eleanor, Put Your Boots On'. More rock songs follow and are eventually broken up by 'Fade Together', another ballad, similar to the first in that it channels psychedelic-era Beatles surprisingly well. There are perhaps two rock songs too many but all are strong. Kapranos dispenses his 'I'm on the road' wisdom from the hip, and in a voice edged with ice. Some songs last only two minutes, long enough to showcase the band's sound: adventurous but solid bass and drums; tightly arranged and highly melodic guitar riffs; and a chameleon-like singer, in Kapranos, who can sound pleading, demanding, camp, grand and snotty.

So what do Franz Ferdinand add to the rock story? Their main trick is to challenge the shape of the rock song through tempo change. They bravely splice their songs and career off in other directions. 'Jacqueline', the first song on their first album, starts out as a plaintive acoustic ballad and skews into a howling rock beast. 'Take Me Out', their breakthrough single, starts as one song, almost stops, then re-starts as another. Their latest single 'Do You Want To' – opening line: "When I woke up tonight / I said I'm going to make somebody love me" – skilfully rearranges all the vital parts of the standard hit record. Franz Ferdinand have willingly, with a mad film editor's glee, cut their work. On the fringes of underground rock this may not seem like a startling invention, but it's amazing how linear and predictable most commercial and indie rock is. When you're selling millions of albums, and when your singles and videos are on big radio and MTV, these shifts, these new directions in which a rock song can go, mark Franz Ferdinand out as something fresh and distinctive.

The last track on *You Could Have It So Much Better* is called 'Outsiders'. Suddenly the riff-o-rama of the previous 12 songs stops. It glides on rhythm: a bubbly bass, a glorious synth line, a funky groove. It sounds like nothing else on the record. It's out to please itself. The lyric goes:

We've seen some change
But we're still outsiders
If everybody's here
Then hell knows
We ride alone.

Go boys. Go.

Back to College

The Hampdens' *The Last Party* & Vampire Weekend's *Vampire Weekend*

Who knew the different ways to sing 'Louis Vuitton' and that the French designer's name would appear twice in songs from young bands in the first half of the year? Susannah Legge, from The Hampdens, drawls and drags her Louis Vuitton, as she does many of the lyrics on her band's debut album, *The Last Party*. Ezra Koenig, from Vampire Weekend, has a Louis Vuitton that is more playful, incorporating an upward French lilt that reflects the fresh and confident tone he strikes all through his band's self-titled debut. Vampire Weekend go even further: they sing "Can you stay up / To see the dawn / In the colours / Of Benetton?" The Hampdens tell us "French *Vogue* knows spiders cling to models' faces"; but then, this comes from a song called 'Generation Y', and an easy way with labels and signs – their superficiality and benign incorporation into our lives – is perhaps one of the distinguishing features of smart bands of this generation.

The Hampdens – who formed in 2002 and are named after Hampden College, the centre of action in Donna Tartt's cult novel *The Secret History* (1992) – hail mainly from Perth and are based in Melbourne. Three EPs have preceded their album, while the band has been distilled to three chief members who also do the songwriting: Legge, on vocals, and two instrumentalists, Julian Hewitt and Gavin Crawcour. The album has been produced by the New York-based Victor Van Vugt, a genial and talented Dutchman who got his start doing live sound for Melbourne bands in the early '80s. His impressive résumé as producer–engineer and mixer includes Nick Cave and the Bad Seeds' *The Good Son*, Beth Orton's *Trailer Park* and Sarah Blasko's *What the Sea Wants, the Sea Will Have*. Van Vugt is not a surprising choice for a young band, given his sure hands in the studio and his ability to calm artists' nerves while satisfying record-company expectations. And his New York experience enables him to bring an adventurous, contemporary sheen to an album, which is attractive to Australian artists searching for something more than the meat-and-potatoes live approach of much local recording.

The record's sound is good. There's silky bass, programmed drums, and live drums that sound like programmed drums; synths either squelch and squeak in late-'90s fashion or are banked and layered in '80s mode, and there's tinkling piano and guitar. It's a lush, compact, Europop-influenced production. The early '80s also figure in the record's approach, as it was an era when pop-obsessed young things leapt from the underground, marrying a knowing wit to the brash new tools of Top-40 sound. Bands like Culture Club and The Human League made glassy, hook-laden music that nodded to lyrical sophistication and adventure, while packaging themselves – both in image and on record – for the mainstream. The Hampdens are less subversive, but they are unabashedly a pop group and they have set out to make a pop record.

The first stumble on *The Last Party* is its length. Debut albums have to strive for impact, and having 14 songs all around the four-minute mark blunts first impressions. The fact that almost every one is mid-tempo is a further impediment, and means that the climb of the record is steady but arduous. No two or three-minute songs enter midway through to offer respite and kick the album along. Another hurdle is the lack of melodic and structural invention: the songs revolve around familiar chord sequences and tumble into familiar choruses. The further the band moves from the strict pop formula that makes the first four numbers almost interchangeable, the more enjoyable and interesting it becomes. 'Forget to Begin' benefits from trying less, aided by a chorus that doesn't leap for uplift. 'Far Away' is almost folky, and has tension and a languid beauty that mirrors Legge's delivery and intimate lyric. 'Miami' has drama and an appealing chopped verse melody that sets it apart from the narcotic drift of much of the album's songwriting.

The world Legge presents – partly with an eye on hitting the zeitgeist with song titles like 'Generation Y' – is jaded, partied out and numb, with refuge found in dreams and sleep and the search for love. But 13 songs of it (there is one cover on the album) makes for heavy going. Just as the album has little musical variety, the lyrics are too locked into one mode. Sometimes, the youthful burnout and suffocation is articulated well, as in "At home I keep a bar / It means I never have to travel far / To be near the nearest thing / That's worth the pain it brings". Other times, it goes round in circles and is oppressive. There are five references to 'signs' in the songs and lots of "I don't know" and "You don't know". Something is trying to be communicated, but it clashes with the exhaustion – "I'm young / But I don't belong." Far better is when the small picture replaces the big, as in 'Far Away', where a domestic scene of cool jealousy is beautifully drawn.

Exploring a generational mood is not something on Vampire Weekend's agenda, because that mood has already been internalised and will be expressed by the band on its own terms. They are four 23 and 24-year-olds who met at New York's Columbia University in 2006 and decided to start a group. Their early shows were primarily on campus, before a very quick career breakout through word of mouth and internet buzz. *Vampire Weekend* was released in February, and it joins Franz Ferdinand's self-titled album and Arcade Fire's *Funeral* as the most impressive rock debuts of the past five years. There are 11 songs on the record and it clocks in at 34 minutes. It is one of those albums that startles from the beginning and doesn't let up on surprises or song quality.

The album's hook, and what has garnered so much attention, is the African influence in the music and the fact that uptown white preppy boys have not only attempted to incorporate this, but done it so well. It seems to have started a chain reaction, whereby each instrument and its place in the band's sound has been reconsidered. Drums are sparse and percussive and seldom swing into standard rock patterns, and when they do – on some killer choruses – the effect is strong. The guitar tone is jazzy and light, with running notes and chopped chords played high on the neck. Vocals are clear in the mix. The bass bubbles and is funky, and follows the drums to hammer home the straight sections of songs. And the keyboards – no serious rock piano, please – are playful organ tones. But it is the assembly of these elements that is most impressive: a very neat, exciting fit, with inclusion determined by necessity, fun value and maximum impact. Throw in one last ingredient – elaborate, thick strings in short blasts – and you have a band that has pulled off the trick of not only appearing from nowhere fast, but also sounding like no one else in 2008.

If, however, the confluence of clever New York songcraft and African rhythms does seem familiar, then yes, there are odd moments when the record does sound like Paul Simon's *Graceland*. *Vampire Weekend*, though, has not had the entire African makeover. This is, after all, a group of very talented New York college kids recording in their home city; they are less concerned with ethnicity (though well versed in postcolonial appropriation) than with how indie rock can be informed by the uplifting clarity and dynamics of African pop. The other traces on *Vampire Weekend* are post-punk pioneers of the late '70s and early '80s like The Feelies, Orange Juice, a touch of Adam Ant – and, of course, the group that every East-Coast band of recent times can't get enough of, Talking Heads. That group had an African period of sorts, and David Byrne and Brian Eno made the heavily African-influenced *My Life in the Bush of Ghosts*. There are hints of this in Vampire Weekend, but what they've done is marry it to the sensibility of early Talking Heads. No eight-minute jams here, but nervy, catchy, two-to-three-minute pop songs.

There's also the touch of Byrne in the lyrics: "You've been checking on my facts / And I admit I have been lax / In double screening what I say / It wasn't funny". The phrase "double screening" probably didn't exist in the late '70s, but the rest of it could be his. There's a lot of smartness on the record, telegraphed from the album's opening line: "I see a mansard roof through the trees." Yet none of it is painful or irritating, and the clipped lyrics fit the curves and stop-starts of the song's melodies. Also, hardly anyone does narrative lyric-writing in New York anymore. Byrne, Lou Reed, Sonic Youth and even Paul Simon killed it off long ago, and successive waves of songwriters – through new wave, no wave, post-punk and beyond – have used lyrics more to signal feelings and pull apart rock's language than to do anything so obvious as tell a story. Vampire Weekend's twist on it is to heighten the collegiate aspect of their lives (sweaters, professors, pinstriped men, pure Egyptian cotton, Cape Cod, and names like Bryn, Blake and Walcott) and play it off against the gritty downtown rock scene and the more exotic African flavour of their music.

Vampire Weekend is a classic first album, and what lies ahead to ponder is the follow-up. There is too much bursting from this record to imagine that the band can't make another album just as good. The wonderful surprise will be gone, and imitators will rush in, but they are young and the debut has a thousand strands to explore. The Hampdens have seemingly done the opposite, in that they have hidden as much as Vampire Weekend have shown. The obvious benefit is that they have, theoretically at least, far more to get out of a second album. And there is enough initial promise in *The Last Party*, and its attempt to make cool classic pop, to suggest that they can do much better next time.

Thoughts in the Middle of a Career

Paul Kelly's *Songs from the South*

It can seem futile trying to chase down biographical material on Paul Kelly because, just as he's ducked the glare of mainstream pop stardom, his self-effacement and unease with his past have left the songs to sketch the details, a situation he probably feels comfortable with. The bones of the story are: he is born into a large Adelaide family in 1955; his father dies when Kelly is 13; he begins playing the guitar at 18; and, after a short time studying Arts at Flinders University, he starts to drift. So he's born and raised outside the cultural axis of Sydney and Melbourne, cities he'll live in during his adult life; and he comes late to the guitar, something which doesn't necessarily affect musical potential. In 1974 he's in Hobart, where he makes his first public appearance, performing the traditional folk song 'Streets of Forbes' and Dylan's 'Girl from the North Country'. It can be safely assumed, therefore, that no photos exist of Paul Kelly in satin pants, stacked boots and a glitter top cranking out Deep Purple or Alice Cooper, as most 19-year-olds with a guitar in their hands were doing at the time. And, finally, no matter how battering the winds must have been to send him to Tasmania, the choice of these two songs for his debut shows a remarkable prescience on Kelly's part, in light of his subsequent career.

The next chapter of the biography – and it is astounding that no official version exists – would take in the mid-to-late-'70s Melbourne pub scene, where Kelly finds rock 'n' roll and songwriting (wine, women *and* song, you'd imagine), and a large cast of musicians and characters who play his music and inspire his songs. Out of this come Paul Kelly and the Dots, who make two records, *Talk* (1981) and *Manila* (1982) for Mushroom – albums that Kelly quickly disowns. He loses his record deal, his band, and times must have turned tough enough for him to leave Melbourne and head to Sydney, arriving by early 1985. That journey is chronicled in 'From St Kilda to Kings Cross', the opening track on *Songs from the South: Volumes 1 & 2*, a greatest-hits collection that pointedly has nothing on it recorded before Kelly turned 30. Behind him is a life lived on the rock 'n' roll margins; the price is sunken, watchful eyes and a gaunt face. Now come the great songs.

But first, let's meet the new band. On drums, there's Michael Barclay; bass, Jon Schofield; keyboards, Peter Bull; and on guitar, Steve Connolly. Over the next five years and five albums these musicians, known as The Coloured Girls and then The Messengers, are going to make a massive contribution to the music of Paul Kelly. Lead guitarists are easy to single out for praise, but Steve Connolly's playing is especially impressive, and the stellar stuff starts with three cuts from the breakthrough *Gossip* album (1986). The band will be robust companions to Kelly, taking the honesty and chops they learnt on the pub scene and dousing it with a '60s-influenced new-wave sound; in recording, it will grow bigger and shinier without losing its edge, a difficult task performed by the last member of the team, Alan Thorne. Kelly's luck holds – more likely, it is acumen – and Thorne produces four of the next five Kelly albums. Thorne's live-in-the-studio approach works beautifully for the band, creating a sound that will not only influence future roots-rock bands but, through its directness, sparkle and dedication to the song, will also come to be seen as particularly Australian. Ultimately, it means the records these people made together are timeless.

Once a great songwriter hits a groove, the first ten years are probably going be the most productive, if not the best. Volumes one and two of *Songs from the South* split at this divide, and while the years 1998 to 2008 are bountiful and well represented here, the character of Paul Kelly, the image of him that still lingers despite the passing years, stems from a fantastic run of pop and rock songs on the first volume, covering the period 1985 to 1997. That character – and it is unimportant how close it is to Kelly himself, although his lack of resemblance to the square-jawed lead singers of the day, from James Reyne through Mark Seymour, must have played a part – is appealing both for its comic value and its sharp-eyed take on modern inner-city romance. The Kelly of these gloriously crafted early songs is bemused ('Look So Fine, Feel So Low'), hungry for love ('Before Too Long'), foolish ('Dumb Things'), regretful ('Careless') and, on 'Darling It Hurts' – surely the best song ever about having a sex-worker girlfriend with a drug habit ("In one hand and out the other") – hurt.

Here's a verse from another song of this period, 'To Her Door', from *Under the Sun* (1987):

> *They got married early, never had no money*
> *Then when he got laid off they really hit the skids*
> *He started up his drinking, then they started fighting*
> *He took it pretty badly, she took both the kids*

There is an empathy here that doesn't seem forced, and an eye for detail that is surely one of the finest qualities of Kelly's writing. It's there again in one of his best-known images, a Silver Top bringing the protagonist swinging through the streets, back to his wife. 'To Her Door' has a happy ending; many of the banished men in Kelly's songs don't get a second chance or have such an easy ride home. 'How to Make Gravy' is sung from jail, where a prisoner on the phone to a family member passes on his grief and his gravy recipe for a family Christmas he knows he can't attend. 'If I Could Start Today Again' is even more poignant: the comforting confinement of a family or relationship is suddenly burst by an unnamed 'thing' the singer has done; he yearns to turn back time, to be taken back. And it isn't only in Kelly's imagined worlds that men get into trouble and have to plead their case. Taking Raymond Carver's short story 'So Much Water, So Close to Home', he masterfully condenses the tale of men on a fishing trip who find the body of a murdered girl in a river and then fish on for two days, before bringing the corpse home to an appalled female narrator. Love songs aren't immune, either: in 'Winter Coat', the singer draws memories from an old coat bought with an ex-lover; he is alone, in exile, "freezing up in these cold, cold hills".

It wasn't only pop and rock songs that Paul Kelly offered on his first run of successful albums. 'Bradman' was a surprise: a seven-minute-plus take on The Don's career was not exactly typical material for a popular songwriter in the late '80s. But it was for Paul Kelly, who was brave enough to take on a story the size of Bradman's and attempt to bridge the gap between the traditional ballad and the rolling melodies of his own songwriting. It's a huge endeavour, like trying to squeeze World War II into an hour-and-a-half movie, and some of the writing is a little creaky ("And at the age of 19 he was playing for the state / From Adelaide to Brisbane the runs did not abate"). But the exit, when Kelly realises he is in fact writing a 20-minute song, is graceful: "So let the part tell the whole."

The other debt to repay is to Bob Dylan, who is central to Kelly's songwriting. 'Girl from the North Country' was an understandable place for Kelly to start a lifelong infatuation with Dylan's work. The early songs of the '60s, with their soft-strummed chords and young man's yearning for social justice and love, are seductive and a natural fit for Kelly and a thousand other singer–songwriters. On 'From Little Things Big Things

Grow' (1991), written with Kev Carmody, the melody of Dylan's 'The Lonesome Death of Hattie Carroll' is given an opening line reworked from 'The Times They Are a-Changin'' – "Gather round people, let me tell you a story" – to recount the long fight of the Aboriginal stockman Vincent Lingiari for equal wages and land rights. 'From Little Things' is more successful than 'Bradman', neater and better crafted, and shows Kelly swiftly honing the skills of a fine balladeer and storyteller. Further lessons no doubt came from watching Dylan grow from the early protest songs through the great '70s songs to the late-period *Time out of Mind* tales of lost love and passing time.

The break with the group comes in 1991, when The Messengers are disbanded and Kelly goes solo. In day-to-day life, this would mean upheavals and life changes for the musicians, Kelly included; on a greatest-hits compilation, it's just one track rolling into the next. But you can hear it: how the grit and muscle of 'Pouring Petrol on a Burning Man' (1990) gives way to the breezy and relaxed 'Love Never Runs on Time', from *Wanted Man* (1994), with the Bull sisters on backing vocals, and Peter Luscombe and Bill McDonald starting their long tenure on drums and bass. Kelly becomes a Melbourne recording artist, a move that allows him to pursue his career as rock performer and writer, while allowing him to dive into the musical subcultures that have festered in the city in unending cycles since the mid '70s. So, well into his forties, Kelly stretches out into collaborations, working with different groups and musicians to make the bluegrass and country-influenced albums *Smoke* (1999) and *Foggy Highway* (2005); a self-titled, rootsy-groove record under the moniker Professor Ratbaggy (1999); and a brittle surf–spy guitar album recorded with his resident group under the name Stardust Five (2006).

Volume two, covering the decade from 1998, suggests it took Kelly some time to mould a band that would inspire and do justice to his rock and pop songs. There were false starts, with 'Love Is the Law' sounding cluttered and one or two other songs sounding too comfortable. The arrival of guitar players Dan Kelly (Paul's nephew) and Dan Luscombe seems to have brought a rush of blood. 'Won't You Come Around' and 'Gunnamatta' from *Ways & Means* (2004) leap out with force; the rhythm section of Luscombe and McDonald gallops to keep up, and a sound is forged. It continues on 'God Told Me To' from *Stolen Apples* (2007) and the previously unreleased 'Thoughts in the Middle of the Night'. This band has lasted three albums with Kelly, and you suspect he has finally found a group that can merit comparison to The Messengers. It is a different beast – more contemporary, more boom and reverb – but in essence it does the same thing: puts fire under the songwriter and makes his up-tempo songs sting.

The other highlight of volume two – and it strongly dictates the flavour of the second disc – is a loose group of songs that have nothing more in common with each other than that they tend to be more story-oriented. They're an odd bunch, and can lead you to believe that the further Kelly gets away from himself, and the more outrageous he is, the better he can be. But then, who wants to end up a comedy songwriter? Although he did have an album called *Comedy* (1991) ... In any case, 'Shane Warne' is great: "Each time he came in to bat or bowl / He believed in his powers of total control / Even when he was not in the peak of condition." It's in a calypso style, with guitar, clarinet and congas. 'Every Fucking City' is the hilarious tale of a bickering couple and missed rendezvous set against the backdrop of Europe's capitals; besides being an exercise in split-second observation and delivery, it's a gentle nip at love songs and how relationships tend to end more in farce and anger than in tears. 'The Oldest Story in the Book' and 'They Thought I Was Asleep' are refinements of the Kelly book of narrative songwriting: gentle, melodic, packed with detail yet cut with economy. And 'If I Could Start Today Again' may just be the best thing he has ever written.

None of these songs would be as good or as pleasurable if Kelly wasn't the singer he is. It is – and you sense his often-unenthusiastic self-appraisals are to blame – his most overlooked talent. His singing can be so in sync with a song's action and character that you forget to notice its quality. It rolls off his tongue; there are no growls or yelps, or strange ticks, or Americanisms, or faux-Pommy bits; he hasn't fallen into the horrible trap of so many old and new folk singers who sound like they've just stepped off the boat at Botany Bay circa 1800. In fact, Kelly doesn't seem to be interested in authenticity at all – it just comes naturally to him and it reaches further because of that, to the campfires and the bush, the suburbs and suburban pub, and the inner-city sophisticates. His voice – sly and warm, laconic and sometimes frail – may be the closest thing we have to a national one.

The first response of a musician on hearing Paul Kelly is often to head to the guitar or piano and work out how his songs go. They invite you to do that because they sound easy and approachable. Most of the tracks on *Songs from the South* are like that. Then you think: If the songs are so simple and the ideas behind them so clear, why aren't more people writing like Paul Kelly and sounding as good as he does? And the answer to that is: "They got married early, never had no money / Then when he got laid off they really hit the skids / He started up his drinking, then they started fighting ..."

An Afternoon at Rough Trade

The first Rough Trade record store opened in 1976 at 202 Kensington Park Road, Notting Hill. It was a good year to open a record store, and a good address given the area's association with late-'60s hippie culture, its Jamaican reggae community and its proximity to the centre of town. In 1983 the shop moved around the corner to 130 Talbot Road, where it remains today – stacked as ever with records, fanzines and a full noticeboard, with best-of lists and old photographs and posters, and staffed by people well up on the current developments in every tangent of indie music.

I first went to the shop in 1979. It was a pilgrimage. A trip to London was not complete without at least one visit, and more were needed, as this was a time when stunning releases were coming out of independent labels every week. The shop then housed a label, also called Rough Trade, that released and promoted some of the bands on the scene. Over the intervening years I've dropped by to get records, to play an in-store performance or two with The Go-Betweens, and to just be there and check the pulse – because Rough Trade is one of those shops that, just by being in it, tells you what a city is like. It provides an instant catch-up. So I visit again in late September 2007, on a Sunday afternoon, and walk out with four new releases and a four-CD compilation.

Alela Diane's *The Pirate's Gospel* is a staff recommendation. It's a record with that particular word-of-mouth current under it that comes from people wanting to pass on something special. Diane is a Native American singer–songwriter, and this is her first album to receive a wide release. It was recorded in 2004; the first 650 copies were all handmade and packed by Diane until demand necessitated a more conventional form of manufacture. Her songs are folky, with blues and gospel touches. The songwriting is underpinned by acoustic guitar and a mesmerising voice that catches you from its first breath.

The album is a family affair, in that her father did the recording, her brother plays guitar and her eight-year-old cousin sings. The songs are in the family too, in a sense. There is displacement, a missing mother, babies, as well as the spirited fight to preserve one's identity in a distant city and against a Christian God (or g–d, as Leonard Cohen writes in his latest book of poems). You can imagine this music coming out of a kitchen: people standing around clapping and singing, someone in a corner on guitar or piano, half heard, as the talented daughter lays down her songs about their lives. This is a very strong album, one that will figure high on the shop's influential list of the top 100 albums of the year, and so the current shall continue.

Although attributing artistic influence can be a hazardous undertaking, you can sense the work of Karen Dalton may be known to Alela Diane. Dalton, besides being of Native American descent and an accomplished guitar player, was the possessor of a startling voice, singing folk and blues (though not her own) full of pride and pain. She recorded two albums in her lifetime, *It's So Hard to Tell Who's Going to Love You the Best* (1969) and *In My Own Time* (1971), and was marketed – though to no great effect – as the 'hillbilly Holiday', due to her voice resembling Billie Holiday's. Usually all comparisons to that singer are ridiculous; in Karen Dalton you can hear not only the similarity but also the quality.

Cotton Eyed Joe is made up of recently discovered tapes of Dalton playing in a small nightclub called The Attic, in Boulder, Colorado. The year is 1962, and 50 people sit at her feet knowing she is no run-of-the-mill folk-boom performer. "Karen Dalton was the real deal," writes Joe

Loop, who ran the club and recorded her, in the sleeve notes. The sound quality is surprisingly high as Dalton runs through two CDs' worth of material. The starkness of the recordings, and the bare plucking of the 12-string guitar and banjo, mark this album as one for devotees. Dalton's two official recordings are a gentler introduction. But it's all here: excellent versions of 'It Hurts Me Too' and 'Katie Cruel', her repertoire and style in place years before she hit the studio.

All four of the new albums I buy have the acoustic guitar at their heart. The biggest surprise is Sonic Youth's Thurston Moore, who, with his solo album *Trees Outside the Academy*, has made a likeable record for all those people that struggle with Sonic Youth. He's heightened the songwriting aspect of his music, dropped the electric experimentation of his band and taken it all out to the country with a violin player, low drums and J Mascis (from Dinosaur Jr) on lead guitar. There is a feeling of freshness and lightness on this record, and by emphasising tunes and a softer sound, Moore's made something far more challenging than what may well be going down in the rock cellars back in town.

Tunng live in the country but have London roots, and their album *Good Arrows* is as fine a soundtrack to the city as I've heard. It's twitchy, intimate, paranoid, abstruse, clever and a bit mad. Where the other three albums could have been recorded anytime over the past 40 years, Tunng's could only have come from the past five. The band's hook is their mixing of traditional instruments with laptop beats and blips, creating an iPod-in-the-ear experience that will have you glaring nervously at the person next to you on the Tube.

They are a collective – at present a six-piece – and this, their third album, is the breakthrough. It's a particularly English experience, with echoes of turn-of-the-'70s Pink Floyd and Bowie: creepy voices, creepy lyrics ("We cut our fingers off / To give ourselves extra insights") and cracking tunes. As with the Thurston Moore release, the album's four best songs are sequenced at the front, and it spins off from an opening melodic rush. One song, 'Bullets', is very good, with a marching chorus that just won't leave your head. That's one to sing on the Tube.

Sometimes I buy albums not only for the music. Something else grabs my eye, or there's some quality about the product that says: "You have to have this." In the case of the Karen Dalton record, I buy it as much for the packaging and the fact that I want to hear 50 people in a room in a small town clapping and talking in 1962. In the full-size book that accompanies the four-CD *Love Is the Song We Sing: San Francisco Nuggets 1965–1970*, there is a two-sided full-colour photo of Jefferson Airplane under a tree in a park, and I know I have to buy the whole package. But there are many other reasons too, not least that the San Francisco psychedelic scene of the late '60s is a favoured chapter of rock history, and this compilation – which draws on the usual suspects (Big Brother and the Holding Company, Grateful Dead, Country Joe and the Fish) and others also great but still relatively unknown – is the best summation of it I've found.

No visit to a record store these days is complete without a worrying thought about its survival as you leave. One large chain in the UK announced recently that the record store has to be reinvented, and as part of the shake-up they will be selling smoothies. You can't imagine smoothies in Rough Trade. The shop's too small for a start, and the German and Spanish customers you hear amid the racks haven't travelled this far to be asked "strawberry or mango?" So what do they want? And what is the modern record store? I don't know. But at the door I pick up a copy of the *Stool Pigeon*, an excellent new free weekly; I check the best-of lists for 2006 on the shop's wall. I've touched the rock books on the counter and seen what's on the listening posts, and overheard some hipsters talking to the staff at the counter. I step out of the shop. London sorted.

Worms Don't Dance

Cat Power's *The Greatest* & Beth Orton's *Comfort of Strangers*

To release an album in January or early February is, sometimes, to make a statement. There are two blocks of the year when most records come out: March to June, and September to November. July and August are European and American summer holidays, so little is released then. December is a favourite dumping ground, home to many a bad record hoping to be lost in the rush. That leaves January and February as the one time of tranquillity, the time when a light can be shone on something special. People have not been bombarded yet, so a record can slip through and travel on word of mouth, and if it does 'bite', the artists has the rest of the year to tour it.

Chan Marshall (Cat Power is the moniker for this one-woman band) and Beth Orton have a few things in common. Both are in their mid thirties, and emerged in the mid '90s with records that made an impact: Marshall with her fourth album, *Moonpix*, and Orton with her debut, *Trailer Park*. Since then they have consolidated, but not gone supernova. Both have wandered; both have done good work and bad. Neither is prolific. Now, about ten years into their careers – always seen as a vital point in the arc of a recording artist's life – they have albums out close to each other, in the early part of the year.

Chan Marshall is a most singular person. Her reputation in the music world, beyond recognition of her unquestionably rich talent, is for erratic and eccentric behaviour. Until now this has made her live performances and interviews fascinating as spectacle – for what she will or will not do, in the face of any definition of the normal. She's a black sheep, deep black. The question after a live show is not "How good?" but a tentative "How was she?" Often brilliant, with a voice straight out of a

Capote short story, she is wilful and capable of trampling over her own talents.

For *The Greatest*, she has gone to Memphis and engaged the services of '70s soul star Al Green's former band members. Mabon 'Teenie' Hodges is on guitar, and his brother Leroy is on bass. Teenie co-wrote the classic 'Take Me to the River'. On drums is Steve Potts; he plays with Booker T and the MGs. These are soul heavyweights. Around them are strings, keyboards, sax, and Marshall on vocals, piano, guitar. The intention is a soul album sonically identified with the Hi label, home of a famous Memphis recording studio and a scene that centred on the work of Al Green, and is perhaps best remembered for Anne Peebles' 'I Can't Stand the Rain'. Hi was funky, with powerful songs and a raw, dirt-bucket soul sound. That's the angle.

The first four songs carry the brief. The opener, 'The Greatest', is Chan's noble hymn to herself:

> *Once I wanted to be the greatest*
> *No wind or waterfall could stall me*
> *And then came the rush of the blood*
> *Stars of night turned deep to rust*

Followed by this breath-taking couplet:

> *Melt me down*
> *Into big black armour*

It's a manifesto on a par with Antony and the Johnsons' 'Hope There's Someone', serving the same purpose: a giving of the heart that is sung over a gorgeous piano lead. 'Living Proof' and 'Could We' (with brass) swing, and are a magical fusion of Marshall and the soul sound. With 'Lived in Bars', the sister to 'The Greatest', it's a quartet of songs so good you'll think you're looking squarely at the new *Dusty in Memphis*. And then it trembles and falls. The countryish 'Empty Shell' is the first crack. It brings in a melancholia that will run deep through the album, like a second stream, dissolving the fine work of the soul songs. It's telling that 'Empty Shell', 'The Moon' and 'Hate' ("I hate myself and I want to die") are all guitar-driven songs. Marshall's guitar skills are not on par with her piano-playing; the melodies are less inventive and, stylistically, at a complete remove from the soul songs.

There are two albums here. With 'Willie' and 'Love & Communication', the soul part makes up six songs. The deeply melancholic guitar side, which has another country number and a breathy, sparse ballad, runs to six songs too. They don't meet. Lyrically they talk to each other, but musically the gulf is too wide. This is a soul album on the one hand, and a Kurt Cobain solo album on the other. Both parts are powerful, but it's the wrong mix. You want the soul album to sustain: the best songs are there and she's got the band. Perhaps we have to go back to the words of 'The Greatest': "Aiming for something with great ambition, but then … the rush of the blood … turned deep to rust."

Focus is not a problem for Beth Orton. She has gone to New York and hired Jim O'Rourke as her producer. O'Rourke is hip; so hip Sonic Youth asked him to join. He made a number of good, influential solo albums in the late '90s, filled with hypnotic guitar-figure songs. Since then he has carved out a role as producer, often working with bands with a more mainstream lilt than himself, such as Wilco. It's a bold choice for

Orton, considering the strength of the 14 songs she has written. Big names would have loved this job, but O'Rourke is an inspired choice.

Comfort of Strangers is out to impress. The songs are strong and the recording process sounds spontaneous, as though the tracks were done in one or two takes. This is no criticism: the playing is so good, so tight, and it's beautifully recorded. Analogue, but dry. It's a record where you can crank the volume up to hear the lyrics, yet it doesn't get harsh.

Orton is engaged right from the outset. "Worms don't dance / They haven't got the balls" is the album's audacious opening line. The first three songs each clock in under three minutes, and all are sure-fire. It's as if she doesn't have to linger over anything, because the next song is going to be just as good. The album is folky, but far too sophisticated to be content with any of the genre's pat formulas. It's easy to fake a reasonable folk album, and Beth Orton could do it as well as anyone. But she challenges herself with the confidence of the freshly liberated. 'Countenance' is pop; 'Shadow of a Doubt' is West-Coast rock; 'A Place Aside' and 'Safe in Your Arms' are moving ballads, centrally placed; 'Shopping Trolley' is indie rock.

The words tumble out of her: funny/sad ruminations on love, meetings and family. None of it too hippie, but with a hippie code, the late '60s to early '70s code of 'love 'em and leave 'em and the journey goes on'. She's smart and tough with it, though. Perhaps it's the London girl in her – a pocket full of songs, doing the American album and succeeding.

And yes, there's something of the *Swordfishtrombones*, *Achtung Baby* and *Blood on the Tracks* about all of this: the artist unexpectedly shedding an old skin and achieving the breakthrough. As so often, the key is simplicity: the long-sought-after alignment of an artist's root worth with the means of expressing it. The lyrics often signal the change. Artists suddenly vomit up tonnes of them, more often than not to brilliant tunes, which feeds back into the singing, super-confident in its newfound strength. Genius often sounds relaxed, as it does here.

This is the album you're going to hear in cafés all year. The prairie voice with the tales to tell. And Chan Marshall? Her time will come. She just needs to work out who she wants to be.

Sunshine on My Brain

The pop genius of The Monkees

Sometimes I play a game in my head: name the five best American rock bands of the '60s. My list goes: The Velvet Underground, The Byrds, The Beach Boys, The Doors, and then I stall on the fifth. Creedence? The Band (although they're mostly Canadian)? Simon and Garfunkel? Jefferson Airplane? The Lovin' Spoonful? But I plump for The Monkees. Song for song they are the best pop group of the period, and their story is one of the most intriguing. The myth that shadows them is that they couldn't play, they weren't really a band and their music was sugary Top Ten fodder. Yet the excellent reissues of their first four albums with bonus discs, released by Rhino Records in the past couple of years, show a band with real depth – one that not only crystallised the very best qualities of West-Coast pop but also pulled off one of the greatest inside coups in showbiz history.

The bones of the group, its talent and temperament, go back to the two men who put it together. Bert Schneider and Bob Rafelson, who hatched and pitched the idea of a television show based on the wacky antics of The Beatles in *A Hard Day's Night* and *Help!*, were West-Coast hipsters with the pulse of the '60s beating within them. Their offbeat approach meant that the four actors/musicians they chose to play the band members in the series were not going to be the square-jawed, Brylcreemed types who usually played anyone under 30 in the TV shows and movies of the time. Those they picked from the 437 applicants to the *Variety* ad calling for "four insane boys" sealed the fate of the band, the show, the music and all those who worked with them. Put simply, if almost any people outside of Michael Nesmith, Micky Dolenz, Davy Jones and Peter Tork had made up The Monkees, we would now have only a slim greatest-hits album to evaluate from a show that might have lasted a year.

The casting net was thrown wide. Tork was a Greenwich Village folkie, Nesmith a wry Texan singer–songwriter, Dolenz an LA-based former child actor, most famous for playing Corky in the late-'50s TV series *Circus Boy*, and Jones was an English-born Broadway singer with roots in vaudeville. That was the band. Actually, it wasn't a band initially because they were only actors playing a band, but then life began imitating art and they became a touring and recording group beyond the one they were hired to be, and they kept their name, The Monkees. So, if nothing else, long before MTV, *American Idol* and every 'reality' show blurring on-and-off-camera life through the prism of mass entertainment, The Monkees were pioneers. And this being the '60s, and with the corporate screws not yet so down on the younger generation, the band had room to wriggle and rebel, leading to some fantastic music, some eye-popping TV, and finally a movie named *Head* that starred Frank Zappa and Victor Mature and began with the four Monkees busting a police cordon and diving off a bridge to their symbolic death.

The first four albums of their squashed (1966–70) recording career can be neatly cut in two. *The Monkees* ('66) and *More of the Monkees* ('67) are straight-up pop albums from what could be called the 'fabricated' era, when the instruments were mostly played by studio musicians and the production and direction of the records was out of the band's hands. Notwithstanding this, both albums are crunchy, hit-laden collections of great songs. There's a ridiculous number of hooks, and an exuberance and glee that is forever tuned to the golden pop of the last half of '66. *The Monkees* has about six potential hit singles on it, yet only one was released: 'The Last Train to Clarksville'. *More of the Monkees*, which followed very swiftly, has 'I'm a Believer' and '(I'm Not Your) Steppin' Stone' (later covered by the Sex Pistols), plus 'Mary Mary', 'She' and 'Look Out (Here Comes Tomorrow)' as further hits – if only there had been time to release them.

What separates the band from their one-hit garage-band and proto-psychedelic contemporaries is that they had a television show to push their music and a corporate music-business structure built into the show that delivered a constant flow of top-notch pop songs. The man behind this, and in some senses the villain of the story, was an old-school music-biz heavy from the East Coast called Don Kirshner. He was the musical supervisor of the first two records. He liked songs with girls' names in them. He discouraged the band's involvement in the recordings, aside from their singing, but had a good ear and fantastic contacts: a horde of Brill Building songwriters struggling in the singer–songwriter world of mid-'60s pop. Kirshner brought in Carole King and Gerry Goffin (responsible for the sublime 'Take a Giant Step' and 'Sometime in the Morning'), Neil Sedaka and Carole Bayer Sager, Neil Diamond ('I'm a Believer'), and David Gates, later of Bread. On the West Coast he had Tommy Boyce and Bobby Hart, members of the LA band The Candy Store Prophets (what a name!), who wrote the show's theme song and a host of killer tunes, including 'Last Train'. And finally there was the stellar songwriting of Michael Nesmith, who by this time had already written 'Different Drum', later a hit for Linda Ronstadt, and who went on to write a dozen very strong songs for the band.

The Monkees had two geniuses: Nesmith and Micky Dolenz. Dolenz is the great unheralded white male pop singer of the era. Top-40 singers before him sound arch and histrionic; Dolenz purrs and glides, skating the curves of a song's melody with a knowing confidence yet able to raise his voice and push and scream – he did a James Brown medley in Monkees concerts – and then pull back to a whisper. Listen to 'I'm a Believer'. Nesmith is a different kettle of fish, and to list his qualities and achievements is to wonder how they could all be contained in one person. For a start, he's a country-rock pioneer: his '66 recordings for the band have banjo, fiddle and steel guitar jangling and bouncing amid the usual guitars and drums. He's a master songwriter who went on to have a fine '70s album career, capped by the hit single 'Rio'. He was a music-video producer and director who in '81 won the first Grammy for a video. He was the executive producer for the film *Repo Man*. He wrote a novel (*The Long Sandy Hair of Neftoon Zamora*), ran a large home-video distribution business and is now an internet guru expounding knowingly on virtual reality and Second Life. Back then, though, he was in The Monkees and causing trouble. It was he who demanded that they become the band they were pretending to be, play their own instruments and take control of the records coming out under their name.

For all the discussion that follows The Monkees, and the very keen criticism they received at the time for their supposed fakeness and plasticity, you wonder how many of the bands with their revolutionary rhetoric on full blast would have held a television network, a record company, an entire hit and money-making machine to the fire in the name of artistic control. And the answer is: very few. But The Monkees did. Nesmith and Tork, mainly – the two musicians of the band – demanded the band choose the material for their records and play it, or they'd quit. The legacy of their move is *Headquarters* ('67) and *Pisces, Aquarius, Capricorn & Jones Ltd.* ('67), the group's third and fourth albums. Perhaps they don't seem too different to the first two records, but there's a unity to their sound and a perceptible wind-down in the search for hit singles that signals The Monkees' shift to being an album band. There is still the gloriously rich mix of songwriting and there is still the sound, a big warm studio mix of live instrumentation at the exotic end of the pop scale. But there is a voice here, hard won by four young men who in making two classic albums became the Frankenstein's monster that walked.

Prejudice towards The Monkees reigns supreme. Nesmith still curses the fact that audiences his own age just don't get the group. Yet if the music they made is dismissed, often on the basis of the singles only, then a closer look at the people around the band would lead you to believe that something was certainly going on beyond a one-dimensional pop outfit and a TV show. The Monkees were a product – but not only of corporate television culture. They were also the product of an LA-based scene explosion, when people involved in rock and pop, film and television, drugs and art, gathered around the city from '65 to '75 to push a younger and wilder voice into mainstream American culture. Peter Tork's house was one of the prime hangouts for the LA folk-rock scene. Schneider and Rafelson went on to produce *Easy Rider* and *The Last Picture Show*. Rafelson directed *Five Easy Pieces*. Jack Nicholson co-wrote *Head*. Tim Buckley and Jimi Hendrix got their first mass exposure through the band, and Micky Dolenz could be spied in full American Indian regalia at the Monterey Pop Festival. With friends like these, The Monkees just have to be fabulous.

I'm looking at an online petition. It's to get The Monkees inducted into the Rock and Roll Hall of Fame. The fools that run this institution are obviously inclined to the old position that The Monkees just aren't rock enough or hip enough to be inducted. The situation is the reverse: The Monkees are too hip for the Rock and Roll Hall of Fame. They have skipped free, the same way they jumped off that bridge back in '68, and are outside rock history. But still, the next time you're thinking of adding a record or two to a collection of classic rock albums, get *Headquarters* or *Pisces, Aquarius, Capricorn & Jones Ltd.* and put them up beside The Byrds' *Younger Than Yesterday* or The Velvet Underground's first album, because it is where they belong.

In Search of a Songwriter

It's lonesome out there on the prairie. There are eagles up in the sky, and birds, lots of birds, and lakes, and wolves, plenty of wolves, and rivers, branches and trees, and even the odd bee. The songwriters that describe this landscape are urbanites who may not feel comfortable in nature but are happy to refer to it and the early-'70s song styles and sounds that accompanied the first golden age of music that brought together the rock world and the great outdoors. Back then it was called country rock or cosmic country, and it included everyone from The Flying Burrito Brothers to The Nitty Gritty Dirt Band, Jerry Jeff Walker to Waylon Jennings, to those denim kings of the cash register the Eagles. Then it faded, as the fashion passed, and everyone cut their hair and shined their belt buckles and played it *way* straighter. The past ten years have seen a re-engagement with both the era's music and its mother-nature muse. And where once the gaze was post-'60s comedown, with plenty of dope and whisky to knock off the edges and keep the beat loose, the current crop has forsaken the cowboys and their ladies and the good times past for a more neurotic and charged reading of the landscape itself. So there are rocks and valleys and rivers, and songwriters in their twenties and thirties investing these words with new meaning to the sounds found in the hippie record collections of their mums and dads and turned-on, layabout friends.

One of the larger homes of this music in Australia is Spunk Records: established in 1998, it has a large and hip roster of local and overseas artists who operate in the indie-rock market. Most of the acts sell hundreds or a few thousand copies of each album, but a high turnover of releases and breakout successes, such as Arcade Fire and the Yeah Yeah

Yeahs, have ensured the label's health and a situation where it often has as many records coming out in a given month as its distributor, the music-industry giant EMI. Spiritually, Spunk is a throwback to the '70s, when record companies were run on the taste of their managers and A&R departments and financed by big sellers, and the vibe was artist-friendly. The economics of the music business have destroyed the large-scale model of the major labels, but niche markets remain, pumped by low-cost recording, vinyl sales, constant touring and the propensity of the artists involved to release albums every two years to an audience eager to follow the twists and turns of their favourite songwriters. Bill Callahan, Bonnie 'Prince' Billy and Wagons are all on Spunk, and benefit from the freedom and indulgence the system provides: it means Callahan has been able to develop as Smog and then blossom under his own name; Wagons have made their best album on the fourth attempt; and the prolific Will Oldham, under the Bonnie 'Prince' Billy banner, has made one too many albums in far too short a time and crashed badly.

Sometimes I Wish We Were an Eagle is Bill Callahan's second album since he dropped the appellation Smog. He resides in Austin, Texas, and his career has taken him from acoustic-guitar home recordings, through electric instruments, band line-ups and recording studios, to the lush instrumentation and widescreen shimmer of his current album. It has been a journey to watch, and the success of *Sometimes I Wish* comes not only from a strong and pointed set of songs, but from the placement of Callahan's dark baritone voice in a pool of sound that is sweet and uplifting. The effect is of beauty coating the beast, and is redolent of those terrific late-'60s recordings by booze-ridden, gravel-voiced actors such as Richard Harris and Lee Marvin. Callahan's earlier wry, monotone delivery did have its pleasures, and seemed to have found a home amid the minimal folk structures of *A River Ain't Too Much to Love* (2005). Here, though, he has thrown the dice, artistically and probably financially, and brought in a string section and some lovely guitar playing to enrich the songs and find new places for his voice to go.

Not that Callahan is easy or accessible, a would-be-mainstream artist. There are too many idiosyncrasies layered in his music for him to hope to gain the late-'60s AM-radio success of prime Glen Campbell or Bobby Goldsboro, which in instrumentation and sweep *Sometimes I Wish* echoes. And that's the lovely core of this record: the vibrant re-creation of a grand, string-driven and twangy-guitared era of pop playing off against a songwriter happy to croon "It's time to put God away" over and over through the verses of a nine-minute song. At heart Callahan is a minimalist, in lyric and in melody; he uses repetition in both so his songs are taut and razor-sharp. On this album the melodies are particularly good and the lyrics punchier and funnier: "I ended up in search of ordinary things / Like how can a wave possibly be?" Add the cream of production, and Callahan has made his best album so far.

He and Will Oldham are often bracketed together as singer–songwriters; both gained recognition in the mid-'90s and have grown from raw early albums made in a tortured folk style to a classicism of song-craft and sound that hasn't chipped away character. And while Callahan staggers his releases so there is at least the sense of a breath taken between albums, Oldham – recording under the Bonnie 'Prince' Billy moniker – ploughs on, racking up five studio albums and three EPs since 2006. Some of the work is collaborative, but the workload is punishing nonetheless. He possesses a fine musical mind, and even in the turbulence of so much released work can imbue each album with a sense of place and intent. *The Letting Go* (2006) was an austere, string-driven collection of songs recorded in Iceland; *Lie Down in the Light* (2008), a warm set of folk parables made in Nashville. *Beware*, from its sound and design, was intended to be a joyous, full-band record that kicked Oldham out on the road to do the press interviews he usually avoids, and a long run of touring. The first and last songs, 'Beware Your Only Friend' and 'Afraid Ain't Me', fulfil the brief; the trouble is that everything between them sounds tired and has been bettered on previous albums.

Oldham needs a break from the studio, and no amount of cute tricks – be it glockenspiel and trumpet solos, handclaps, phased '70s-country guitar or choirs – can cover up weak melodies or what are for him exhausted song genres, such as the country ballad or the spooky folk tune. The two strong songs are sturdy and big-chorused, and an album built on them would have been another step in Oldham's career; unfortunately, he has either not given himself the time to write the remainder of the album in their style, or has been happy to have the best numbers as bookends to a set of songs that back away from their challenge. By 'There Is Something I Have To Say', song 10 of 13, with the singer yet again mournfully chewing over the failed communication between him and his partner, accompanied by a plucked Spanish guitar, it's time for someone else to come on down the highway, some band with a spring in their step who know how to wrap the mysteries of the universe – and that includes warning off musicians trying to 'crack on' to the singer's sister – in an album that runs to just 33 minutes and 3 seconds flat.

Wagons could only have come from present-day Melbourne or a farm outside Sunbury circa 1974. They are a satirical country-rock band, far broader than the poker-faced Callahan and Oldham but with a heart and skill to their songs that pushes them beyond being a comedy act. They are led by Henry Wagons; and, as with all deep-voiced singers, from Johnny

Cash to Tex Perkins and The Handsome Family's Brett Sparks, when you get down to the crooning register it can become a marvellous weapon in playing the straight a little crooked and the crooked a little straight. *The Rise and Fall of Goodtown* is not a concept album, but all the concerns of the country-rock suite are lovingly covered, from the lure of the roulette wheel ('The Gambler') to the mess a bewitching woman can make of a man's mind ('Evette') to the simple hedonistic joys of being in a band ('Drive All Night Till Dawn'). There's a touch of Nick Cave and the Bad Seeds in 'Love Me Like I Love You'; but Wagons, besides owing a major debt to the '70s, have managed to filter and master enough of their influences to cut fresh ground for themselves, and make an album that's short and sharp and very entertaining.

It has been a quiet and unspectacular start to the year, with no hot breakthrough bands, such as Vampire Weekend or Fleet Foxes were in 2008. Bruce Springsteen, Morrissey, Franz Ferdinand, Neil Young, to an extent Antony and the Johnsons, and now Bonnie 'Prince' Billy have all made albums that have failed to meet expectations. Nothing seems to have caught fire; certainly no singer–songwriter is cutting through in a big way. Bill Callahan's *Sometimes I Wish We Were An Eagle* will deservedly be on best-of-the-year lists: he's made a very fine record. Something is still missing, though – some new songwriter willing to stake out new territory and leave nature well enough alone. Or, as Henry Wagons succinctly puts it: "Why do we talk about the birds and the bees / When one is in the flowers and the other is in the trees?"

Too Smart to Run Back

Allo Darlin''s *Allo Darlin'*

The history of the ukulele in rock music is as short and quirky as the instrument itself. Before pop music there was cheeky Englishman George Formby Jr strumming 'When I'm Cleaning Windows' – "for a nosey parker, it's an interesting job" – and then into the flowered late-'60s charts strolled the talented Tiny Tim, with his make-up and curls, baggy suits and ukulele carried in a paper bag, singing 'Tiptoe Through the Tulips' and other vaudeville and Tin Pan Alley hits. In the rock world the 'uke' was enjoyed mostly in private, George Harrison being one enthusiast, and when Paul McCartney wished to pay tribute to his friend on his latest tour, he did so by playing 'Something' solo on ukulele. The instrument has been a staple on the alternative cabaret and roots-music scenes, enjoying a further burst of popularity with the banjo, kazoo, toy piano, mandolin and other decidedly non-rock instruments in the indie folk world over the last years. With perhaps none of this in mind the Rockhampton-born Elizabeth Morris visited the Duke of Uke shop in London's Brick Lane in 2005 to buy a ukulele and soon discovered that the limitations and feel of the 'uke' opened a door to songwriting that had been closed to her on the more traditional song-crafting instruments of piano or guitar.

The songs she has written since then are the foundation of Allo Darlin's eponymous debut album. Joining her is Bill Botting on bass, who was in the Brisbane band Polyvinyl, and on drums and guitar two Englishmen from Kent, Michael Collins and Paul Rains – Allo Darlin' are based in London. The music they make is indie pop, a simple label but one hard to pin down in an ever-expanding indie scene that gobbles up genres and spits out mutations at a furious, internet-geared rate. Allo

Darlin' are the way much indie music used to sound, a style born of the more melodic and guitar-oriented end of post-punk, which was sugar-coated in the late '80s by labels such as Sarah Records, and then perfected into popular form in the mid '90s by Belle & Sebastian with their first three albums. Over the last ten years the twee pop scene has had to fend for itself as the young hipsters ran off and raided other closets. The White Stripes, The Strokes, Arctic Monkeys and Animal Collective weren't interested in writing about wistful glances exchanged between sensitive souls on the last bus home. Allo Darlin' have picked up an old baton, and their record gives pleasure not only because they have revisited a recognisable sound with dash, but also because there are many good songs here, well written and imaginatively played.

The first impression the album gives is of lightness and sweetness, qualities not in vogue and not usually associated with either depth of feeling or musicians attentive to sonic detail. The obvious star is Paul Rains, who plays beautiful guitar. He underpins Morris' melodies with tuneful jangle and fuzz, and helps to carry the first four songs along with a momentum that has you landing at song five, the album's first ballad, 'Heartbeat Chilli', as if having undergone a speedboat ride and been delivered windblown to a distant shore. To welcome you are the slow chopped chords of Morris's ukulele and the song's opening lines: "I was in the kitchen on my own making chilli / You came in with an onion and got dicing." As an opening side of an album it is nothing if not impressive.

And it is not only Rains who is committed and inventive. Michael Collins began drumming in Allo Darlin', and though it is detectable in his playing, the effect is charming and never detrimental to the songs. A missed beat at the start of 'Kiss Your Lips' is startling to hear in an era of instant digital correction. Other bands would have shifted the accent, but Allo Darlin' don't, and that dropped beat and the speeding up at the end of some songs is a microcosm of the band: joyful, natural and far too smart to run back and correct mistakes.

The album was recorded in the summer of 2009 at Soup Studios, which in a neat twist of fate is located under the Duke of Uke shop. The songs chronicle the four years from instrument purchase to recording, and lyrically it's a London album, lived by someone in their twenties. There is the everyday: the lack of money, long faces on the Tube, the heightened pleasures to be found in the night from a city that can grind you down by day, and beneath all this beat the myths you surround yourself with as you struggle and triumph in a foreign city. A lot of the songs centre on affairs of the heart, and Morris, perhaps by temperament and certainly in line with indie-pop dictates, is modest and romantic. The sound and approach of the album is aligned with its lyrics. There is a pre-Beatles, pre-1963 ring to much of the record: a naivety in the rhythm section, the tremolo in the guitar, and Joe Meek-inspired echoes in the production. Morris's direct and relatively simple lyrics chime well with her melodies and the girlish tone of her voice, and offer a contrast to much of the agony and over-writing to be found in the first recorded works of many of her contemporaries.

Two songs near the end of the album stand out. The narcotic pull of lap steel guitar and throbbing bass helps lift 'Let's Go Swimming' away from London to a lake near the Swedish coast. This is a song about the influence of landscape on inner feeling, and after seven songs around love it's good to get out on the water. Morris doesn't rummage too hard for meaning, letting the three verses arrive with whatever associations they may bring; some are straightforward – "the water here is so clear I can see to the bottom" – some funny – "it feels new to go swimming where nothing can eat you" – and some poetic, as the water throws her back to the waves of "a central coast of Queensland" childhood. It's the only Australian reference on the album and it is powerful because it is unexpected and small. 'My Heart Is a Drummer' follows, and like 'Let's Go Swimming' it takes away from the effervescence of the opening tracks. It is the only number on the album that gets inside a relationship, and the rebuke and the tension in the song give the album a deeper dimension as it reaches its close. There is also a misstep or two. 'Woody Allen' is too sweet, with "In the movie of our lives would Woody Allen write the screenplay?" as its opening line. And a slow chorus of Doris Day's 'Que Sera Sera' in the record's final song, 'What Will Be Will Be', is a quote too many on an album with its fair share of references.

Generously thanked in the album's credits is Allo Darlin''s engineer and producer Simon Trought. He deserves it: this is a beautiful-sounding record. Low-fi to some ears, the album bypasses the dense harsh sprawl of much small- to mid-budget modern recording to go for a sound that's in tune with the band's instrumentation and that respects the need for audible lead vocals on lyric-intense music. He also integrates Morris's ukulele to fit the band – and not the band to fit the ukulele – so that the thick strum of the instrument goes in and out of the album as exotic rhythm, reminding us where the songs have come from.

Many bands make big, broad debut albums and their second efforts are often retreats. Allo Darlin' the band with *Allo Darlin'* the album have shot lower and hit higher, and now have open doors before them. The fashion wheel could turn too, and the kind of spirited 'old-school' indie pop Allo Darlin' make may be next year's hot ticket – another reason, if one more were needed, to pay attention now.

Welcome to the New Neil

Neil Diamond's *12 Songs*

Neil Diamond and Rick Rubin are like two trains meeting, having come from opposite directions. Diamond is the veteran: 40 years in the business, hit singles, Vegas, movies and 'You Don't Bring Me Flowers' with Barbra Streisand. Rubin is the hip record producer: Red Hot Chili Peppers, Johnny Cash's last four albums, System of a Down and the Run-DMC and Aerosmith smash 'Walk This Way'. Two guys from different sides of the tracks, but together they've done it. At 60-plus, with Rubin by his side, Neil Diamond has cut an album he can be very proud of. There are gold singles on his wall; platinum-selling albums, too. Yet with *12 Songs* he's thrown a real punch: probably no hit singles, just a sustained cycle of songs that crowns what at times has been a tinsel career.

Between 1966 and 1971, Neil Diamond wrote 20 great pop songs. He managed to match Brill Building, pre-Beatles songwriting skill to a post-Dylan singer–songwriter 'auteur' voice and throw it high into the hit parade. It was a stunning run of singles. 'Solitary Man'. 'Girl, You'll Be a Woman Soon'. 'Shilo'. 'Kentucky Woman'. 'I Am ... I Said'. 'Cracklin' Rose'. Plus 'I'm a Believer' and 'A Little Bit Me, a Little Bit You' for The Monkees. All his, all with his mark. Simple chords masking a sophisticated musical brain. And an equally brilliant lyric theme: the lonely guy, suspicious of love but dying to fall into it, warning girls of the shallow traps of other men; at the same time, willing to sing his heart out for any woman he loved.

So whatever came after this – the glitz, the sequins, all the trappings that a big American career that runs to middle age can bring – at the beginning was a brilliant songwriter. And it's back to the beginning that Rubin has gone.

Rubin is an interesting character. He looks like the kind of guy you see in coastal caravan parks: scraggly long hair, full beard, wizard eyes, dispensing wisdom to young surfers around the surf club, drawing the older crowd around the fire at night. In the conservative rock world of LA, he's an oddball, but one with power, success, and an ear and an eye for music that has him choosing projects that vary from young million-sellers to older artists comfortable with a maverick. Johnny Cash answered the call, happy to talk esoteric religious belief and have his career and life turned around. Diamond evidently needed some convincing before being won over by Rubin's notoriously seductive bedside manner and the hope of creating what must have seemed to be the one missing jewel in his show-business crown: the great album. And Diamond, in his mid-sixties, may have thought: How much time do I really have left?

In an interview Rubin referred to Diamond as "Springsteen, before Springsteen". Diamond, in his wonderful accompanying sleeve notes, describes the listening sessions both of them had before recording started, "like two teenagers". Diamond wanted to hear early rock 'n' roll. Rubin went to Diamond's early work, quizzing him, leading Diamond to listen to his own first recordings. Perhaps it was out of this that one vital change came. Amazingly, since the late '60s Diamond had not played guitar on any of his records. Rubin put him back on guitar and with one stroke made him a singer–songwriter again.

The album begins with 'Oh Mary'. Straight up it's there: no theatrics, no grab at the throat. Diamond counts in. Strummed acoustic guitar, deep piano notes, the voice high up in the mix. It's almost a folk song. Rubin's strategy is immediately clear: a big talent is ready to reveal itself; no frills, none needed. 'Hell Yeah' follows. It's Diamond's 'My Way', but don't let that put you off. Again the sound is stripped back. The song climbs through its three-chord frame to a bloodcurdling octave leap by Diamond in the last chorus. As an opening nine-minute ballad double-hit, it's perfection. And the sound is a canyon: all natural, crystal acoustic guitars, '70s rock-ballad piano, organ and warm bass.

'Captain of a Shipwreck' comes as a breather. It's good, though – Gordon Lightfoot could have written it. Then comes 'Evermore'. If 'Oh Mary' and 'Hell Yeah' were hills to climb, this is Mount Olympus. It starts off simply. Diamond and his guitar, and then – as so often in his work – he gets into a rhythm on a chord, and a different melody comes in, anthemic yet restrained, and the song builds. And here's Rubin's genius. No synthesiser pads or crashing drums, but a warm, liquid build-up of piano, bass and then strings. Natural instruments taking the weight and driving the song to three-quarters of the way in, where the orchestra swirls, ready to take on Diamond's rhythmic melody. Diamond pulls back and then implores, "Why, tell me why, oh why?" This moment, simple words over a gorgeous orchestral wave, is maybe, just maybe, the greatest Neil Diamond moment of all time.

From here, the rest of the album is a sterling retreat from dizzy heights. Rubin is sequencing, though, so there are tricks to play and different sides to show. 'Save Me a Saturday Night' and 'Delirious Love' are the pop numbers. The first, if done at twice the speed, could be a Monkees hit circa 1966. But Neil's older now and there's a warm crack in his voice as he sings:

Save me a Saturday night
Leave me some room at your table
Slip into your heart if I might
And stay just as long as I'm able

It's retirement-home pop. 'Delirious Love' is the closest this record gets to 'old' Neil Diamond, and it's a deliciously hyped-up version of it. The theme of the song seems to be new love as orgasm, or the closest any person can get to explaining it in song.

This is the album's halfway point and from here the tone becomes darker and more clipped. It is a bold move, sustained by a series of songs about love and close friendships. Diamond, with typical certainty, unflinchingly covers it all. It can get a little gruelling, but relief comes with the arrival of the cute ragtime pop of 'We': "Love is not about you / It's not about me / It's about we." And so ends the album.

Rubin has taken all the bluster and bad heat out of Diamond. He's done this with production decisions: there are no drums, the backing is minimal but always tasteful (vibes, slide guitar, Billy Preston on organ). Diamond never seems under-accompanied. One could accuse Rubin of stacking the better tracks in the first half of the record, but then he probably thought he had a lot of convincing to do out there in rock-hipster land. And what will the old fans think – the ones who groove to 'Sweet Caroline' and 'Forever in Blue Jeans'? You know, they might just like it, even if they find it a little mournful.

With Diamond, you always have to bring a bit of belief with you. Nothing is ever done by halves, and he can get schmaltzy – his wordplay can rely too heavily on the stock-in-trade. But I love the reach and the man can write a tune. In rock-speak, for decades 'Neil' has meant Neil Young. But with Young on a long holiday from creativity and Diamond suddenly proffering something as strong as this, well, it has to be said: it's a late changing of the guard. Welcome to the new Neil.

Frank's Back

Frank Black's *Honeycomb*

This is a Sunday afternoon barbecue record: people milling about, sausages turning, maybe some Mexican beer. "Who's this?" someone asks. "It's the guy who used to be in The Pixies," someone else replies. There are blank looks until another person, the owner of the record perhaps, adds: "He's gone to Nashville and made a country album with some famous old players. Sounds good, doesn't it?" And it does. People nod, the dog barks and *Honeycomb* drifts nicely around the garden encircled by the picket fence.

The sleeve credits pronounce that "no digital manipulation was used", and the sound is lovely, warm and rich, picking up every lick those old players – Steve Cropper, Reggie Young, Buddy Miller, pianist Spooner Oldham – lay down. It's the dream team a record collector would put forward if asked to assemble a band. And in a roundabout way, that is the album's pitch: alternative rock god cuts loose off-the-cuff album with super-respected A-list older guys he digs.

For the most part it works. Black's voice breaks and croaks and can then go pure honey. His songwriting is professional enough and inspired in places – 'I Burn Today' and 'Sing for Joy' – while other songs roll and move in ways we have heard before. His strength is melody, his weakness lyrics, which tend to match first-thought rhyme with irritating stream-of-consciousness logic. The three covers come with mixed results. Do we really need another version of 'Dark End of the Street'? But it's almost as if *Honeycomb* is operating on another level. The concept works. It's not background music and yet it slides easily into the background, with a classic '70s feel, so that back at the barbecue someone is saying, "Isn't this a great record?" – and you think, Well, not really, as you reach for another beer.

Distant Sounds

Various Artists *Community: A Compilation of Hobart Music*

When is Tasmania going to produce some great bands? It must be soon, if only through the converging of cultural forces, time and the fact that both Brisbane and Perth have had a fruitful past decade of breakthrough artists and bands and the frontier needs a new place to shift to. Writers such as Robert Dessaix, Nicholas Shakespeare and Richard Flanagan are already there, the $75 million privately owned Museum of Old and New Art is set to open on the shores of the Derwent, the Falls Festival hosts a great line-up of artists at Marion Bay each year, and even rock royalty is on the trail, with ex-Violent Femmes bassist Brian Ritchie relocating from New York to take up, among other things, the curatorship of a local music and art festival.

So what's there, and what does it sound like? Answers lie with Julian Teakle, Hobart's resident guru and member of electronic duo The Native Cats. He has compiled a 19-track collection that acts as a guide to the city's indie music scene, an ever-changing and interlocking world of which Teakle hopes he can "capture a few still moments in this constant state of flux". On first hearing, what defines the compilation is not what is included but what is not: a slew of bands playing catchy, fast, hook-laden pop hoping to win favours at Triple J. Perhaps there are bands such as these in Hobart or neighbouring towns, making Vampire Weekend/Franz Ferdinand/Fleet Foxes-influenced variants on what constitutes young modern pop, but *Community*'s 73 minutes is broad and inclusive, and the music for better or worse takes its time and wanders in a state of blissful endeavour, creating a body of work far different from similar compilations in any of the mainland major cities.

Two strains of music, or two approaches to music-making,

predominate: the band, and the lone singer–songwriter working at home. The bands tend to be big-sounding, brutal even, with post-rock leanings. The songs are all group compositions, and the lack of songwriter voice or vision tends to make much of the music run too predictably along the lines of whatever genre the band is focused upon. So The Love-In's 'Hitting C' and The Que's 'Fern Tree Recording Excerpt', though tense and 'grooved', are five-minute-plus one-note 'jams', roughly in the Sonic Youth style. Moe Grizzly's 'Stereo/Lowlife' is too close to Joy Division's 'Transmission', and Hey Mook, who are easily the most traditional rock band on the record, just get their heads above their Neil Young/Church influences on 'Southerly Bluster'. It should also be noted that, as ever, the bands with the strangest names often make the least convincing music: such is the case here with Drunk Elk and Paint Your Golden Face.

Two groups stand out. Ivy St's 'Bright Eyes' is very 1981, with bludgeoning bass and hysterical vocals, but it is powerful and confident and melodically well grounded. All Fires the Fire push the year of influence to 1984, with the addition of synthesisers and Adam Ouston's moody vocals, and make much of an era not noted for likeable music. Both these groups have a hint of bleak northern England about them, the doom-y, 4AD Records aura of dislocation and imposing landscape that perhaps has found a resonance in the winds and winters and outlook of Hobart.

Isolation and distance and the options and opportunities available at that distance must play a part in a compilation like this. With the spotlight off and a small sprawling port city to negotiate, bands and artists rely on a sense of co-operation and tolerance to survive and flourish. Artistically, though, that is a double-edged sword: isolation and its gift of an added sense of self can benefit the creative process and sharpen an artist's work, while the lack of a wide and critical audience eats at the feedback the artist or band needs to develop and bounce. Things can drift – strange, wonderful talents may grow in the dark – while distance and its imposing lack of urgency may cause others to lag behind. All of this is magnified in the hands of solo artists, and *Community* showcases a wild posse of songwriters recording at home or in small studios and sending their music out to friends and a wider internet world in search of bite, feedback, or even fame. This is where the compilation gets more interesting, tracking a set of songwriters with nothing to lose.

There is no knockout genius here – no Bon Iver or PJ Harvey figure lurking in the wilds somewhere. The strangest and most beguiling songwriter on the record is perhaps also the straightest. Liam Constable's arpeggios on the Spanish guitar may set up a familiar introduction, but his first verse sung in a strine-ish Australian brogue is an eye-popping confession: "Unable to quench our pathetic desires / Loneliness plagued us with a great sense of urgency / We caught each other with our pants down / We saw each other's ugliness and we failed to look away." With this shock in the air, the song then glides into a beautiful chorus that delivers the song's title, 'I Truly Care for You', with total sincerity. It's mesmerising and, along with the icy synth walls of All Fires the Fire, the best moment on the album. Constable works so well because of his avoidance, intentional or not, of many of the gestures that infest indie rock, and there are plenty of them on this album – though some are done quite well. Our Sails's 'Notes from a Fighter' is fine wonder-pop from the Grandaddy/Mercury Rev school. Billy Whims and The Vivids both do high-voiced, cute indie pop; the latter's 'Tighten Up

Your Skates' recorded and mixed "in a cubby". And Teakle's own band The Native Cats proffers not only a strong song, 'Little Me Belongs to Little You', but with its whiplash minimalism a lesson in inventive low-fi recording. The band's vocalist, Peter Escott, who seems to be the town's provocateur, has a solo career and 'Every Inch of You Is Gold' is him alone on reverbed piano; it is demanding and unusual and better than anything on his *Slow Coach* album.

Teakle does this trick often, of pulling a performance or a song from an artist's catalogue that shows them at their best. *Community* is no quick grub. It is well sequenced and exposure to the artists' own albums reveals the discernment and care in his choices. Ivy St's recently recorded 'Bright Lights' is stronger than anything on their debut *Picture Machine* album. All Fires the Fire's 'Headlights' is the pick of their six-track demo from October last year. 'So It Goes' from Billy Whims is the lead track of her *What We Made* album and a fine introduction to her work. It is also easy to spot Teakle's desire to expose the tangle of band members and recording set-ups: this is a scene, and the fact that Anthony Rochester recorded seven of the bands and plays drums in The Love-In, and members of one band record another, and that the long thank-you lists on the albums are always thanking the same people is seen as a strength and charming feature of what is happening around Hobart.

And if there are no gold records to be had, or thousand-strong audiences at gigs for local bands, or Sydney A&R scouts crawling around practice rooms, there's at least attitude and pride. A jocular defiance is encoded in much of the music and spelt out in the press notes from Teakle that read less as straight record-company information and more as wry-eyed manifesto: "We scoff at your concern about our cold weather and supposed isolation, and revel in the rumour that Victorian premier

John Brumby spent a weekend down here not long ago, caught a few shows at the Brisbane Hotel and the Alley Cat Bar, and is at this very moment drawing up plans to drop Melbourne somewhere in the middle of the Baltic Sea for a couple of years to try and achieve the same effect. It'll never work. You can't manufacture this kind of talent."

He's right, you can't – it's all too wilful and eccentric, the crush of artists and their distant world making the appealing *Community* not dissimilar to compilations by early-'80s English indie labels such as Cherry Red or Rough Trade (*Community* is on the homage-sounding Rough Skies Records). These were labels that pulled disparate artists together, some acts experimental, some acts closer to mainstream pop, all glued to a particular label and somehow evoking identity. Both of the British labels were run by music-loving men with a vision, and so out of *Community* comes not only a portrait of a city through its recording artists, but also a clear sense of the hand of Julian Teakle, which may in time be as influential as the music he is collecting and making.

Love Goes to a Building on Fire

The Shins' *Wincing the Night Away* &
Clap Your Hands Say Yeah's *Some Loud Thunder*

There's a conundrum faced by certain bands, successful indie-rock ones especially. If the first album or two have broken through and lifted the band above the horde of contenders, should the band continue operating on their current level, which has brought them this success, or should they use the success to try to reach the next rung on the show-business ladder? Record company or management pressures aside, what does the band *want* to do?

The Shins and Clap Your Hands Say Yeah, both out of the US, are in this position. The Shins are a four-piece from Portland, Oregon, having started life in the more remote New Mexico. *Wincing the Night Away* is their third album, and they're on the perennially hip Sub Pop label, out of Seattle. So it's a West-Coast operation, which immediately separates the band from Clap Your Hands Say Yeah, who are from the East Coast (Brooklyn and Philadelphia), are on their second album – *Some Loud Thunder* – and have their own label. The bands play different kinds of music, too, which also neatly reflects the coastal divide. The Shins are a pop band: curling melodies, a radio-friendly lead voice and not-too-disconcerting lyrics about the boy–girl situation. Clap Your Hands are pure New York, noir and difficult, the latest in a long line of bands that reference The Velvet Underground. Both bands have successful albums behind them, and both have reached the same conclusion: get the producer.

For Clap Your Hands Say Yeah, the decision is more surprising. Given the sonic range of their music and its roots, they could have stayed in town and made an album like their last. They haven't gone too far, though: up the road to Dave Fridmann's studio in upstate New York. Fridmann has been an in-demand producer for adventurous bands with a budget for some time. His client list reads The Flaming Lips, Mogwai and Sleater-Kinney. His masterpiece remains Mercury Rev's *Deserter's Songs*, one of the very few great rock albums of the last ten years. As a choice of producer, it's understandable and definitely a step up.

The Shins have also looked close to home, coming up with experienced and adaptable LA craftsman Joe Chiccarelli. The record company mentions Beck and U2 as his clients, but skips Elton John, Bon Jovi and Chicago. No matter; he would have been chosen for his safe hands and ability to calm and polish artists wanting to sell records but still wishing to hold onto their 'art'.

The Shins' rise has been measured but steep. Their debut album, *Oh, Inverted World*, came out in 2001; *Chutes Too Narrow*, the follow-up, was released in 2003; and now, four years later, comes their third. *Chutes* was always going to be a hard act to follow. It's a very good album: ten beautifully arranged pop songs based primarily around the acoustic guitar. Its success, though, seemed to have more to do with an aura floating around the record – the singular vision of James Mercer, the band's singer–songwriter, who, with his boyish angelic voice, built a world through his songs that people rushed to inhabit. It was hushed and intimate, like diary entries, but backed by solid, real-world pop smarts. The album broke them out of indie world and set them up for a shot at the mainstream – if they wanted it.

The gap between recordings has allowed the band time to make their decision and prepare for the assault. The results are radical. Gone is the classic indie production of *Chutes*; in its place is the smooth, thick, synthetic sound of major-label pop. The twist in this – the out-card, if you like, for the band – is the record's loving embrace of the '80s. It's as if Mercer and co.'s jump to the mainstream can be facilitated, encouraged even, by a warm clasping of The Smiths (very noticeably here), U2, some Cure and early Crowded House. The production decisions and the sound go hand in hand with this, which helps explain the old-school choice of Chiccarelli. For fans, it's a shock; for the new audience, the welcome mat is particularly shiny.

And what of the songs? They're strong; the ones on *Chutes* pip them, but Mercer is too good a songwriter to let his side of the bargain down. The more important matter is what the sound does to the songs. The first and most obvious thing is that Mercer has been pulled back into the band, both in his vocals and in his presence. His voice has lost its adolescent tremble and he now sounds more like The Cure's Robert Smith, detached and lower in the mix. At the same time, the drums have come up and acquired a noticeable '80s-style whack. The electric guitar has all but overtaken the acoustic, and has a distinct Johnny Marr ring to it, right down to the tremolo touches and snaky minor-seventh flourishes.

The effect is distinctly chilling. The band sounds removed; the collar-grabbing freshness has been replaced by ambient pop. And for the most part, it works. *Chutes*, for all its brilliance, had them in a corner, and trying to remake or fake its naivety would have been fatal. So they've set out for a new sound, one that weds the next phase of their musical development to their commercial aspirations.

Over on the East Coast, it's a different story. For Clap Your Hands Say Yeah, commercial considerations are not so important as establishing a career as a credible, close-to-the-edge rock band. The way to do this is to stay the course, making well-judged adjustments to their sound (hence David Fridmann) while banking on their songwriter to consistently produce quality material. It's what worked on their debut album, where one good track galloped into another; it's the lack of a steady flow of strong songs that lets *Some Loud Thunder* down.

The five good ones on the record are those that are more poppy and melodic: these the band's singer–songwriter, Alec Ounsworth, can write and write well. It's the other sort of song that's the problem. He has various stabs at constructing things that might break up or angle off from his strengths, but none of them is good enough. More worryingly, most have a pretentious, getting-clever-in-the-home-studio feel to them, which acts as a further turn-off. 'Satan Can't Dance' is a flat 'funky' anti-dance song; 'Arms and Hammer' tries too hard to be a strange folk tale; 'Love Song No. 7', with Ounsworth's voice multi-tracked, sounds like Supertramp. Only 'Upon Encountering the Crippled Elephant' (it's weird-song-titles à go-go with these guys), a short and pretty waltzing instrumental, manages to construct something that links the fine pop songs together. And the fine pop songs really are marvellous, twisting, inventive takes on post-Velvets rock.

A barrier to the band, all but ruling out broader success, is Ounsworth's voice. It comes in two broad guises: Gordon Gano of the Violent Femmes, and David Byrne; the shadings are Television's Tom Verlaine and Dylan circa '64, the 'It Ain't Me, Babe' era. It's not often that you can characterise a singer by naming so few influences, but Ounsworth swaps so freely between his inspirations that it almost creates a vocal style in itself. He also uses them on songs that recall the bands whose singers he sounds like. So the quicker-strummed, wound-up numbers have the nasal whine of Gano, while the more laid-back numbers – or the quieter sections of songs – have the Byrne croon. The similarities with the latter are so close that 'Over and Over (Lost and Found)', on their first album, sounds like *the* great lost late-'70s Talking Heads song. And being a Talking Heads obsessive, it was this number that first drew me to Clap Your Hands. Its simple two-chord elegance and uncluttered post-punk approach are missed on much of what they've done since.

Neither of these albums is a complete success. The Shins have lost too much sparkle; Clap Your Hands Say Yeah are in the studio too early, and haven't managed to reach that desperately needed next stage. So, two of the more significant indie hopes for early 2007 fall short. Of course, market forces may take over for The Shins, who are a pop band and have certainly made a pop record. But Arcade Fire, Kings of Leon, Art of Fighting and other big shooters are on the horizon, with records coming soon. Salvation may lie there.

Slippin'

AC/DC's *Black Ice*

In the beginning, back in 1966, there was Harry Vanda and George Young. They were the songwriting team in The Easybeats, responsible for such riff-heavy pop classics as 'Friday on My Mind' and 'Good Times'. George Young had two younger brothers, Malcolm and Angus, who in their early twenties wrote a series of riff-laden rock anthems, among them 'Jailbreak', 'High Voltage' and 'It's a Long Way to the Top (If You Want to Rock 'n' Roll)'. George knew the singer and larrikin supreme Bon Scott from Bon's '60s band, The Valentines, whose biggest hit, 'My Old Man's a Groovy Old Man', he co-wrote with Harry Vanda. George helped Bon join his younger brothers' band, AC/DC, a group built on the solid bricks of family, '60s pop history and the search for the perfect guitar riff. Young and Vanda's other service was to produce the first six AC/DC albums, before handing the job to the London-based 'Mutt' Lange, who began a run of three albums with *Highway to Hell* (1979) – the last to feature Bon Scott as the band's singer and lyricist.

The death of Bon Scott, in February 1980, is the one stinging note of tragedy in the AC/DC story. The band has sold a phenomenal number of records, can headline stadiums at will, and has seen the cream of their songs enter rock history. But when Bon died, the Young brothers lost a wild and wise older 'brother', and a singer and stage performer who could ride the beefy riffage coming from their guitars. *Back in Black* (1980), which has now sold 22 million copies in the US alone, was then a tentative step out with a new singer, Brian Johnson, in tow. If there was a morsel of grace in Bon Scott's passing, it was that he lived long enough to help forge AC/DC's style and sound, but briefly enough to allow Malcolm and Angus, then in their mid-twenties, to write some of the finest songs of their lives. *Back in Black* stands as the best AC/DC album and is central to the group's mythology of endurance and rejuvenation, of lean, tight rock 'n' roll and shaking All Night Long.

Black Ice comes 28 years later, and eight years after the last AC/DC album, *Stiff Upper Lip*. From the title and packaging's echo of *Back in Black*, the band, if not saying such a groundbreaking moment has arrived again, is at least signalling a significant career juncture. Perhaps it is seen as the start of stage three, after the Bon Scott years and the long run down since *Back in Black*. As with the arrival of 'Mutt' Lange in the late '70s, AC/DC has turned to a name producer, Brendan O'Brien, known for pop hooks and a chunky contemporary sound. Hailing from Atlanta, O'Brien has made Pearl Jam albums and worked with other hard-rocking bands, such as Velvet Revolver and Audioslave. He can also handle singer–songwriters, and gained further prominence for his work on the last couple of Bruce Springsteen albums – another artist who loves a big sound, even if at times it is to the detriment of his songs. So *Black Ice* sounds like an AC/DC record. The drums are higher in the mix and the singer may have come down a touch from the early '80s albums, but then, in O'Brien's hands everything sounds loud – and on an AC/DC record, that's how it should be.

One thing O'Brien has not been able to do – assuming he tried – is to maximise the album's impact by keeping it near the classic 40-minute mark. *Black Ice* is the longest AC/DC record ever; perhaps, after eight years, the Young brothers thought they had a huge cache of new ammunition to fire. They don't. Poor songwriting lets the album down. There has always been an if-it-ain't-broke ethos in the band that reflexively rejects any criticism of the simplicity and grunt of the melodies, or the limitations of the sound. But good AC/DC songs, besides their signature blend of guitar riff and chords, have hooks and originality, and in a lot of the '70s work humour and drama, and in something like 'Hells Bells' (off *Back in Black*) a creeping progressiveness – all of which are in short supply on *Black Ice*'s 15 songs. The reduction that goes into an AC/DC song, and the tight palette of influences the band has always worked with, gave the early work precision and power, but three decades later it acts less as liberator and more as noose, especially when the band is attempting a late-career kick-off.

The strongest songs on the album are the first and last. 'Rock 'n' Roll Train' is a great opening shot. There is air and dynamics here, as instruments tumble in knowing there's a classic song to deliver. It has the one anthemic chorus that is fresh and, with Angus Young's guitar solo rearing up before the second chorus, it is the one punch on the record that you don't see coming. The three songs that follow maintain the momentum, while gesturing towards a diversity that never materialises. 'Skies on Fire' is built on a good grinding riff; 'Big Jack' contains the other great chorus on the record; and 'Anything Goes' is a pop song, the most un-AC/DC thing attempted this time around.

Then comes the tumble. Pack your bag with plenty of water for a long walk across the desert: tracks 5 through 14 are tough going. There is numbing predictability in melody, sound, instrumentation, song length, lyrical content, vocal delivery and everything else that goes into a rock song. Small, tantalising hints of variety are offered, then quickly snatched away. So we get a bit of slide guitar at the start of 'Stormy May Day' and a verse of lower-register singing. 'Rock 'n' Roll Dream', the album's only ballad, at least changes the tempo – at song 13. Nimbleness and invention finally return with the album's title track and closer. The previous half-hour of relentless chug and uninspired boogie is suddenly cut off by a snaky, Zeppelin-style riff that opens up the verse–chorus structure, giving the song a bounce and vigour the preceding ten songs lack.

Besides offering two tracks that could make it on to a best-of collection, the album's most notable feature is a group photo inside the booklet. They look like a nice bunch of guys. There is openness and humility to their faces, and a sense of comfort with each other that doesn't come across in their music – not on this record, anyway. The 2008 AC/DC has wrought one good change: a noticeable toning down of the nasty degradation of women that was so prevalent on the early albums. Unlike *Back in Black*, there's no 'Givin' the Dog a Bone' or 'Let Me Put My Love into You', with its rape-fantasy chorus, "Don't you struggle, don't you fight, don't you worry because it's your turn tonight" and parting line, "Let me cut your cake with my knife". Still, in the lyrics that are decipherable – and because of Johnson's high-pitched, garbled wail, a lot aren't – there is little correlation between what's being sung and the lives of five wealthy middle-aged men. 'Spoilin' for a Fight'? 'Smash 'n' Grab'? A fantasy is being maintained and sold, and the fans expect it and love the band for it. But if AC/DC is looking for ways to grow and survive, which writing songs and releasing an album indicates, then words are needed that match the band members' hard-won age lines, and their smiles.

There is someone in the photo who isn't smiling, of course. He's got his lips curled in a practised scowl. That schoolboy uniform he's worn since the band's early days is still there, although it's been subtly altered over time – a bit like the wearer. There's no satchel now, no school crest, as if the significance of the costume is slowly being bled out of it. If Angus Young is ever going to escape, though, at 53 he is leaving his run pretty late. From the stadium seats, the twitching legs and flailing arms coming out of the short pants and jacket are probably plausible, and so central to the AC/DC spectacle that they can never be dropped. And as rock 'n' roll gimmicks go, it's a great one. But it's also a trap, and the older Angus gets, the sillier it looks. A black T-shirt and a pair of jeans are waiting; so is the next great AC/DC album.

God Save His Soul

The Sleepy Jackson's *Personality: One Was a Spider, One Was a Bird*

It happened the old-fashioned way, by hearing the single first. 'God Lead Your Soul', it's called. You play it once and think, That's a strange record, and then find it doesn't leave you. You come back the next day and play it twice, and it intrigues even more. So you try and unlock its charms, its whereabouts, almost. What is this record, this glorious slice of circa-1970 country-pop that begins as if in the middle of the song, and then continues to shift across the musical landscape like a Western stagecoach – harmonies, pedal steel, a brass section from the late '60s all coming in, and yet none of it, bizarrely enough, with the imprint of retro upon it. The song's good, and it's been carried through these production styles to create something otherworldly and precious, and miles from the punch of much contemporary music. It's the work of Luke Steele, he of The Sleepy Jackson, and it's the first shot of a man going out on a limb, consequences be damned.

The Sleepy Jackson came out of Perth in 1999. They released two well-received EPs, and then *Lovers*, their debut album, came out in 2003. As career positioning, it all seemed perfect. The album got ecstatic reviews, then ARIA nominations, and the international press sat up and took notice. Here was a young band with a charismatic lead singer and songwriter ready to go anywhere. *Lovers* charted in the UK, the band toured, but, as often happens with successful young musicians on the road, things started to fray. Members left, management got tangled, lawsuits and bad blood followed. After the giddy trip, Steele found himself alone (a recurrent word on this new album): the captain of the ship, as always, but with no one around him to command. *Personality* was born of these circumstances. It's the fight out. The work of a man on a mission – chips on both shoulders, God behind him – convinced he can make a masterpiece.

The album's setup is almost a pastiche of a pop epic. There's a 24-piece live orchestra, percussion, vibraphone, banks of harmonies and choral arrangements, plus the usuals: synths, keyboards, bass and drums, and up to four guitarists on some songs. It's all there, a sumptuous blend heralding the confidence Steele has in his own songwriting. All of this is fuelled by the very interesting 'personality' of Steele, who is almost a parody, at times, of the eccentric, messianic pop star. He has created an alter ego called Luke Blonde (Steele in a blond wig), who runs the Church of Harmonology; there are photos with clocks and other props, slogans written on hands, and a whole run of attention-seeking pop behaviour that's both a cry for meaning and a way for him to psych himself into total self-belief. He's got that, and he's set out to make that very rare beast, hard to find on the Australian major-label roster (but often dreamed about by the bedroom songwriter): the big-budget, soaringly ambitious, experimental pop album.

His choice of cohorts and location in this endeavour is interesting. Steele, for all his cosmic intentions, seems to prefer things local. He still lives in hometown Perth. No big-name overseas producer on the record, but rather Scott Horscroft, part-owner of and engineer at Big Jesus Burger Studios in inner Sydney. Horscroft is an intriguing choice for Steele to make at this stage of his career: no obvious big-hit maker, but a composer, sound artist and musician with avant-garde leanings. The studio is an analogue-equipment paradise. Steele's gone for authenticity and naturalness, tinged with the possibilities of the 'out there', a place where he believes his visions and dreams of the songs can be brought to life. A place, also, where he will remain in control.

There are 13 songs on the album and it comes in at a crisp 42 minutes. One can be thankful that Steele doesn't have a taste for progressive rock, because with music this grand it could expand and bloat to anything. His love of pop and the hook keep him in line and the album focused. Steele's great talent as a songwriter is as a melodist. Part of his gift is pulling strong choruses out of verses, and they flow with no feeling of I-need-a-hit assemblage. His cherished era (at least on this record) is the late '60s and the '70s; his ambition is to put a spin on it and crash it into the future. The songs reference the big boys of pop: The Beach Boys, McCartney, Electric Light Orchestra, the Bee Gees, a stretch to Prince, some folk. It's a generational reshuffle, weeding out some of the more iconic artists of the past for a reappraisal of those once deemed a little un-hip, at the sweet end of the pop spectrum.

The most distinguishing feature of *Personality* is its sound. It was the grab that pulled me in on first hearing 'God Lead Your Soul'. The album is thick with instrumentation; when something comes into the mix it doesn't tend to leave. The mixes themselves aren't dynamic – there isn't the usual pulling-out and highlighting of lead instrumentation and riffs. Everything stays very much in the middle. The album does have a lovely analogy pull-and-tug, but it also starts to feel very heavy and thick two-thirds in. It's an album in need of some remixing, a decluttering and highlighting, lead vocal up, strings coming in and being heard, guitars up or out. Things aren't helped by the large amount of layered backing vocals from Steele that eat up a lot of space. A pop album needs to breathe, and one appreciates the moments of clarity that infrequently arrive.

One such moment is 'Miles Away', a gorgeous strummed ballad. It's spare and cut down; Steele's vocal is thrown high in the mix, where it pulls you right in. Here is engagement, a connection between artist and listener. A piano line on the chorus comes in, and it's the first really effective overdub on the album since the brass on 'God Lead Your Soul'. Lyrically, it is also a welcome break from a lot of moaning and angst over his history and former band-members. Steele gets emotional and it comes as a clear pool of thought. His description of a lost trip across America is poignant and moving: "Couldn't tell you why / Couldn't tell you why I was so cold with you then." He sings over a breath-taking melody, cueing the line, "We still love you at home but you're not here now." It's the album's first real emotional wham, done with ease and class.

'How Was I Supposed To Know?' is similar – though instead of being stripped back it has the full string-driven production – and again an emotional vulnerability shines through: "How was I supposed to know that I was on my own? / Why do I keep telling you I was on my own?" They're the last words on *Personality*, sung to a lover, sung to himself. Past all the bravado, and the biting, and the machinations of the superstar trip, there is the confused boy, mostly hidden on this album, but when he does appear he brings beautiful songs.

Bryan Looks Back

Bryan Ferry's *Dylanesque*

Many years ago there was a show on ABC Television called *GTK*. The initials stood for the rather quaint phrase 'getting to know'. The broadcast ran from 6:30 in the evening and, from memory, lasted somewhere between 10 and 20 minutes. For adolescents such as myself who could occasionally wrestle the television from their parents, *GTK* offered a briefly glimpsed window into youth culture, rock 'n' roll in particular. It was an odd program, in the light of the format-driven, all-information-in-advance entertainment culture of today. Anything could pop up. The show came from Sydney and could swing through fashion, international bands currently on tour, counter-cultural stuff, and local rock news and bands. It was a quick, idiosyncratic and enlightening report that also featured a skilful selection of overseas music clips and films.

Three of these clips remain in my mind. David Bowie in a startling combination of make-up and suit, singing 'Life on Mars' on a white set. Ry Cooder in a recording studio with a live band, playing *Paradise and Lunch*-era funky blues – one of the first occasions I'd seen a group of musicians playing great music together. And Bryan Ferry doing 'A Hard Rain's a-Gonna Fall', seated at the piano in profile, with jet-black hair and black T-shirt, three female backing singers behind him in '30s/'40s garb. It was probably the first time I'd ever seen him perform, although I owned two albums by his band, Roxy Music, and *These Foolish Things*, his first solo album, from which the cover of Bob Dylan's 'A Hard Rain' came.

Ferry doing Dylan in 1973 seemed a strange proposition. Through his slick and flamboyant Roxy persona, Bryan Ferry was at the absolute peak of his influence. In contrast, and at the time in an artistic wilderness, Bob Dylan was the '60s but the wrong kind, not camp or plastic but earthbound and a bit grubby. Ferry, though, pulled off a stroke of genius. With 'A Hard Rain', he took one of Dylan's greatest and most revered early works, a stark and compelling piece of protest-era songwriting, and put it into the glam-rock blender. And by God, it worked. 'A Hard Rain' being a three-chord folk song, Ferry not only saw the possibilities of pounding it into a fantastic three-chord rock song, but the opportunity to add all the touches so characteristic of his work at that moment: grand camp gestures that the song just had to lie down and take.

What also got Ferry, beyond the pleasure of completely reconstructing a '60s classic, was the chance to sing its words. Here was the primary connection. In his own work, and shown in his hip appreciation on *These Foolish Things* of everything from Cole Porter through to Lesley Gore's *It's My Party*, it was obvious Ferry valued the lyric and had a particular take on its history in popular song. So he was drawn to Dylan. He also knew Dylan's supreme gift as a songwriter and a singer, dipping into his catalogue again for 'It Ain't Me, Babe' on *Another Time, Another Place* (1974), his second solo album. And from then on, it's been appreciation from afar, Ferry noting in interviews that he'd never met the great man nor heard his opinion of his cover versions. But even given this initial fruitful crossing back in '73, it still came as a surprise to hear that Ferry, notoriously hesitant in releasing albums and always mistrustful of anything approaching spontaneity, had recorded a complete album of Dylan songs in a week.

First off, nothing succeeds on *Dylanesque* as well as 'A Hard Rain', and to give Ferry his due he doesn't really put himself in a position to try.

This is the record of an older man, knowing that he has already recorded one of the greatest cover versions of Dylan ever, and who is happy to revisit the songwriter's work but in the glow of that achievement. It's not an album that sets out for total engagement, to collar you and scream or whisper its pain or prophecy, as albums of original material often do. Ferry's coolness as an artist comes into play here, too. This is an album you can let play in another room, wander in on and smile appreciatively when he gets it right, and leave on the occasions he gets it a little wrong.

The record begins strongly and surprisingly with 'Just Like Tom Thumb's Blues', off *Highway 61 Revisited* (1965). It's Dylan in his wildest and most fantastically poetical period, the time when he let his hair explode in curls and wrote 'Like a Rolling Stone'. Two other songs on *Dylanesque* also come from this era: 'Gates of Eden', from *Bringing It All Back Home* (1965), and the single 'Positively 4th Street', also from '65. These are big songs to go at, not only because of their monster status in the Dylan catalogue, but also because of the first-time authority Dylan whacked on them. Plus, they are druggy, weird and evocative of the mid-'60s milieu they vividly portray. But Ferry gets under their skin, his trembling voice and the stripped-down instrumentation revealing a vulnerability in the lyrics that the original recordings had hidden. 'Positively 4th Street' is no longer a caustic kiss-off but the rueful pleading of a former friend; 'Gates of Eden' is not a strident song-poem but a gliding, spooky hymn. It is the turning of these songs – from familiar conceptions to something fresh – that is the album's triumph.

One other highlight is 'Make You Feel My Love'. Ferry's atmospheric tears-in-the-rain treatment of this, highlighting the song's latent romanticism, eclipses Dylan's original version on *Time out of Mind* (1997). On that album the song is a little buried, and for once not helped by a

Dylan vocal that fails to fully reach the beauty of the melody. Ferry steps in and gives the song the tenderness and the arrangement it's always needed. His more commercial approach to recording, which he's always had, is a kick against the norm for artists tackling Dylan. Bar bands, singer–songwriters and big rock guns love Dylan and usually mimic his rough-and-ready approach to the studio. So it's interesting to see what Ferry brings to these songs, and it's amazing also how often in the first ten or so seconds you can tell whether or not his treatment will succeed.

In general, the quieter numbers on the album work better than the rock ones. On the more subdued songs Ferry brings the sophisticated Roxy touch, and this makes for an effective and seldom-heard contrast to Dylan's recordings. The louder approach, with Ferry's love of '70s guitar licks to the fore, and the presence of the celebrated '80s mixer Bob Clearmountain and his crashing snare, lands 'Baby, Let Me Follow You Down' and 'All Along the Watchtower' straight in the bin. The inclusion of the latter is bizarre. Dylan's stripped-back original is magnificent; Hendrix's inspired rock cover definitive. Where else can you go? 'If Not for You' also suffers from its Velvets 'Sweet Jane' chug, and anyway, who is ever going to top Olivia Newton-John's gorgeous pop rendering from 1971?

Greyer areas are 'Simple Twist of Fate', 'The Times They Are a-Changin'' and 'Knockin' on Heaven's Door'. 'Simple Twist' is the most overtly commercial turn on the album, and initially the slick treatment it receives – up against Dylan's bittersweet acoustic original – has you gasping. But you find yourself won over; a little like Ferry's hit version of John Lennon's 'Jealous Guy', the song describes a private moment, and laces its melody with radio-friendly production. 'The Times' gets the guitar chug again, and is reminiscent of 'A Hard Rain' in its attempt to remake and remodel an early, dry folk song. It's not bad. And the oft-covered 'Knockin' on Heaven's Door' Ferry stretches to six minutes, with female singers and a good arrangement; the minutes glide by and it's affecting.

This is no earth-shattering record. It's for Ferry lovers and Dylan people – a tossed bouquet for anyone in between. You'll be in a lift somewhere and Bryan Ferry singing 'The Times They Are a-Changin'' will come on, and it will seem kind of funny and appropriate. You'll be in a bar in Lisbon and there'll be a radio playing and Ferry's soft croon of 'Gates of Eden' will float to you. In those moments, this record will seem perfect.

Nature Boy

Antony and the Johnsons' *The Crying Light*

Four years ago, while on a promotional tour for the last Go-Betweens record, I came across Antony and the Johnsons' second album. I was in Amsterdam and had asked our local record-company rep how our album was being received, to be told, in typically abrupt Dutch fashion, "Well – but the album everyone is excited about is this," as he handed me a copy of the yet-to-be-released *I Am a Bird Now*. My first opportunity to hear it was the next day, as I was driven through the streets of suburban Milan. Antony Hegarty's searing voice and the exquisite melancholy of the songs seemed to float up to the apartment buildings I saw out of the corner of the taxi window. It was a singular experience, and one that wedded the first hearing to a landscape and situation from which I can never separate the record. Almost four years later, a journalist friend in Munich tells me that he has an advance copy of the new Antony and the Johnsons album. I travel there to pick it up, and bring it back to the small village in Bavaria where I am temporarily staying. I put on *The Crying Light* and it is the first day of snow: white-covered pine trees as if dipped in sugar, snow on the fields, the sky a clear-cut blue. Again, Antony's voice, another cycle of songs; but this time a new landscape.

The voice is the first thing you hear, tremulous and aching, the four-year wait ending with the sudden reintroduction of Antony's finest gift. He entrances you, as all great singers do, and much of the enjoyment of the album – even in its more demanding moments – comes from the quality of his singing. And the voice is very much at the centre of this record, for where *I Am a Bird Now*, with its fuller instrumentation and illustrious guest singers (from Boy George to Rufus Wainwright), was more of a group effort, *The Crying Light* has the feel of a solo album.

Antony takes lead vocal on all ten songs and his accompanying piano is the one strong musical constant throughout, with the only other major shading coming from Philip Glass protégé Nico Muhly's eccentric and playful string arrangements. This is an album of ballad confessionals, from a singer who can channel Nina Simone and early Bryan Ferry at will, in language that would make the most star-crossed of poets blush.

And it's a very difficult album to judge. The problem is the completeness of Antony's vision and the seal he puts upon it through his singing and songs. The question you find yourself asking is: How does this record stack up against the last one? The narcotic pull of *The Crying Light* means that is a hard judgement to make. When you can extricate yourself from the music, a few insights are forthcoming. Firstly, the last record had better songs. They were more traditional, with clearer pop/soul structures; there will be those who will champion the abstraction of the new songs, but the first five numbers (at least) of *I Am a Bird Now* are simply peerless. Also, *I Am a Bird Now* had a strong narrative and as unorthodox as it seemed to be – the search by someone who describes himself as transgender for sexual identity and self-identity – the quest, the cry of "Who am I?" has always had a place in music, rock music especially. *The Crying Light* lacks the once-in-a-lifetime run of songs, and the joy and wonder that came from hearing Antony's high, honey-toned voice for the first time. But he is tenacious and smart – those who find fame in their mid-thirties usually are – and the four-year gap between albums seems part of a considered retreat before releasing a record that is surprising in both subject matter and delivery.

For all the differences between albums, *The Crying Light* has a similar shape to its predecessor. Ten songs clock in at just under 40 minutes, with better songs first, before a slight trailing off and a return with a poignant, great last song. The mood, though, is all, and where *I Am a Bird Now* went out to greet and grip, the new album is coiled and inward-looking. This has its charm, but it's a slow burn. The song that should start the album, 'Kiss My Name', with its kick and chorus, is track four – coming after three ballads. But it's more than that: it's the delicate haiku-like lyrics, the sheer sparseness of the sound, and the vision which is contemplative and mysterious and close to that most inward of all things, the heart. It is also telling that one song which could have broken the spell, 'Shake That Devil', an up-tempo bluesy romp, was left off the album to grace the 2008 *Another World* EP.

In interviews Antony has said that he writes songs in cycles. The *I Am a Bird Now* songs, staggeringly enough, date to the mid-90s (which is a long time to sit on classics); a second, as-yet-unreleased cycle exists from the late 90s; and the songs for the current album were written after 2001. This explains the punch of the *I Am a Bird Now* material, as the first good songs of a songwriter often have a uniqueness and directness that can be hard to recapture. The gap also explains why *The Crying Light* and its predecessor don't talk to each other in the way that successive albums usually do. (And it is to Antony's credit that he has not taken the more recent songs and tried to force them into the mould of the previous successful record.) Finally, Antony is based in New York, and the *Crying Light* songs sound like much post-September-11 art: sombre, quietly spoken, yearning for serenity, and focused on big symbols tied to the source of peace and order and renewal – in the natural world.

A key song, and the album's single, is 'Another World'. It is the sixth track and a simpler, almost anthemic distillation of all that has come before: "I need another place / Will there be peace? / I need another world / This one's nearly gone." This is the core of the record and it is no surprise that the only goodbyes offered in the following verses are to the trees, the sun and the animals. It is hard to remember an album so fixated on the elements and so devoid of everyday human touch; when people or spirits enter, they are evoked in such over-dramatised language that they are almost abstractions. 'Daylight and the Sun', which follows, attempts to kick the morbidity, bursting in with "How I cry for daylight" as an opening line. At six minutes it is the longest song on the record, and once again restoration and refuge are linked to nature. It is as if the sensitivities that once gave voice to the anguished longings and confusions of sexual identity can now only turn to human survival and retreat, with this no better encapsulated than in a verse from 'Everglade', the gorgeous final song: "When I'm peeping in a parlour of trees / And the leaves are winking all around / 'I'm home,' my heart sobs in my veins."

This is a beautiful album, and those coming to Antony and the Johnsons for the first time will find it glittering and arresting and it will appear like nothing else on the horizon. Antony's song-poems will beguile, and his voice will melt you. But for those who know and love *I Am a Bird Now*, *The Crying Light* will be elusive. It is far more an art-based album; the strings winding off after the end of songs, the absence of bass and drums, the bizarreness and strong poetry of the lyrics all attest to that. And in a way, it's a burning-off of ambition, too, or perhaps that is what it will seem to those with a more rock or pop orientation. It fits the new landscape, though – perfectly. Indoors, but still chilly. Happy to look at the world in its winter colours.

BOOKS

Pop Producer in B-Grade Movie Actress Murder Trial

Mick Brown's *Tearing Down the Wall of Sound: The Rise and Fall of Phil Spector*

On 23 May 2005, Phil Spector entered a courtroom in Los Angeles to hear evidence to be admitted to his trial for the murder of Lana Clarkson. He arrived wearing a permed ash-blond afro, the top of which stood nine inches from his head. He was nattily dressed in a blue shirt with large gold buttons and a black jacket with silk handkerchief and silver broach. This image immediately flashed around the world. That night the comedian Jay Leno joked on his TV show that Spector "looks like he's already got the electric chair". For long-time friends of Spector the photograph would not have seemed so strange, nor would his wish to appear like this in court. Wigs and flamboyant, attention-seeking clothes have been a part of Spector's wardrobe since the early '60s. The petulant look on his face they would have known too, masking keen intelligence and the fact that he was not in control of the circumstances around him. And finally, they would have known that after all the years of him waving guns around, someone had to get shot.

Phil Spector is a record producer. Actually, you could say he was the first record producer. Jerry Wexler from Atlantic Records, who knew and worked with Spector early in his career, deftly places him in rock history. First there were the producers whom Wexler calls the 'documentarians', people like Leonard Chess who in the '50s recorded blues singers such as Muddy Waters live in the studio. Then there was the more sophisticated pop approach of the 'servant of the project', which is where Wexler puts himself, "whose job was to enhance; to find the right song, the right arrangement, the right band and the right studio ... to bring out the best in the artist". And then came Phil Spector, who co-wrote some of his artists' songs and worked with the same musicians in the same studio to create a signature sound that varied little from record to record. This is the 'producer as star, as artist' category, and Spector is the starting point.

His main acts were The Ronettes, The Crystals, The Righteous Brothers and Darlene Love. The songs are 'Be My Baby', 'Da Doo Ron Ron', 'You've Lost That Lovin' Feelin'', 'He's a Rebel' and so on. It's a very hefty body of work, and it has a royal place in pop history. This is the sound of 1962–63: a massive wash of instrumentation and arrangement with a lead vocal wailing over the top, usually about a boy whom the singer has just met and wants to marry. It's pre-Beatles and pre-Dylan, the last big gasp of innocence before the '60s rush it all away. It's candyfloss hair, the Kennedy administration, big voices and simple choices: "He walked up to me / And asked me if I wanted to dance." And it's magnificent.

Spector was born in the Bronx, New York in 1939, and most of his recorded work was done in Los Angeles. The tug between the coasts, his travels and loyalties to both places, drive his life and the narrative of Mick Brown's book (Bloomsbury, 2007). Spector's father committed suicide when he was nine. His one sister was schizophrenic, his mother was domineering and his parents, both from immigrant Jewish-Ukrainian families, were related (perhaps first cousins) before marriage. As a family knot it's wildly overheated, and the manic, sensitive, preening, precocious boy who projects himself into the LA music scene of the late '50s was the result of it. His first hit, and still the best song he wrote on his own, is 'To Know Him Is to Love Him' – a gorgeous love song, but a chill lies in knowing that this was the epitaph on his father's gravestone.

By late 1961 Spector had his whole operation in place. He did it by turning the same motivation and talent that had got him out of his family and into the pop charts to his next goal, to be a record producer. He blitzed both coasts, taking what he could get from whomever he met. So he co-wrote 'Spanish Harlem' for Ben E King, played guitar on Leiber and Stoller sessions, and produced a few singles. Importantly, he also gathered mentors. Atlantic Records chief Ahmet Ertegun, songwriter Doc Pomus and West-Coast promotions man Lester Sill all dug the crazy kid with pop dreams. It was Sill who set up the Philles record label, the first piece of the empire. Spector had the studio (Gold Star), the musicians and the songwriting contacts. All he needed was the artists, and those he often stole. And after that came the sound.

What Spector makes of its famed description is not in this book. But nevertheless 'wall of sound' is attached to him, the way 'ambient' dogs Brian Eno and 'surf music' sticks to Brian Wilson. As a description of what he does it's not bad, although probably the best album Spector has produced, *John Lennon/Plastic Ono Band*, is a minimal bare-knuckle ride that has nothing to do with a wall of sound. But as a demarcation point, and as a sense of how the songs came out of a teenager's radio, it's accurate. Brown, with the help of Larry Levine, Spector's long-time and long-suffering sound engineer, gives a good account of the components and uniqueness of Spector's recording style. Basically, it's three of everything – piano players, bass players, guitarists, percussionists – where the usual was just one. Spector's genius was to weld them together into a coherent but still overwhelming sound, allowing the drummer to conduct and the singer to soar gloriously.

The result, in tracks like 'Zip-a-Dee-Doo-Dah', an old Disney-movie song from the '40s, is astounding. That he could take an old chestnut like this, mould it into something new and make a hit of it shows what he could do with instrumentation and groove. But it wasn't all sound with Spector. He was a brilliant arranger too, able to dismantle the sound and then rebuild it through the progression of a song. The 15 musicians sitting in the studio were not all blaring at once, and this is what stunned others when they saw Spector work: the amount of time he spent refining the players' parts until he not only got the sound but the arrangement he wanted. Because of the primitive studio equipment of the time Spector was in effect recording his mixes live. 'Symphonies for the kids', he called them, and he was right.

1963 was Spector's year. After that the competition got too stiff, especially from Motown, and each record that Spector put out had a question hanging over it: How can this be topped? The sheer drama of the records seemed to build in a limit of how far it could all go. Two big final singles brought down the curtain on the era: 'You've Lost That Lovin' Feelin'', a mind-boggling record that stunned everyone with its length – 3 minutes and 46 seconds, long for 1964 – and its ghost-like beauty; and 'River Deep – Mountain High' by Ike and Tina Turner, which is one of pop's most controversial records and supposedly Spector's masterpiece. Tina Turner screams out of the mix in a song that has one too many sections, and a kitsch lyric: "When you were a young boy / Did you have a puppy / That always followed you around / Well, I'm going to be as faithful as that puppy ..." It bombed in the US, and Spector quit.

Three years passed until a bizarre offer of rescue came, and with it the final meaningful phase of his recording career. The Beatles called him. Well, not exactly The Beatles. Allen Klein, who had hoodwinked John Lennon into thinking he could sort out his financial affairs, suggested that Spector could salvage the unfinished and unhappy Beatles album *Let It Be*. So Spector came over and put the strings on 'The Long and Winding Road', stayed for two John Lennon albums, including *Imagine*, and did *All Things Must Pass* for George Harrison, which explains the great retro-girl-group force of 'My Sweet Lord'. As an unexpected second phase of work it was phenomenal, and equal to the best of his early '60s recordings.

Phase two, though, unleashed his demons. Drinking, bodyguards with guns, Spector with guns, the breakdown of his marriage to Ronnie Spector, three unwanted adopted children, his bottled-up childhood trauma, the head-trip of stardom, years of indulgence of his behaviour – all now came out and ran free. And it was a mess: in Brown's book there are a hundred pages of disintegration covering the period after the Beatles and solo-Beatle work stopped in 1971. Some recording got done, but Spector fired a gun in a Lennon session, held a gun to Leonard Cohen's face and took aim at Dee Dee Ramone. Up in his castle home, a lonely and washed-up Spector – in psychoanalysis, on medication and drinking jags – wallowed and made life hell for those around him. There were personal blows: the death of his only son, aged nine, and being sued for back royalties by The Ronettes and Darlene Love. None justified his treatment of other people.

Mick Brown entered in late 2002 to do the first serious interview in 25 years. He got the full treatment: Rolls Royce pick-up, waiting secretaries, postponements. Spector finally made his entrance, to classical music and in a black silk pyjama suit with silver monogrammed initials. The interview was spectacular; as Brown notes, it was as if Spector had been waiting to get a lot off his chest. And it was pure Spector, a mad, brilliant mix of candour and bullshit in dated hip-speak. There were jokes ("Michael Jackson starting out life as a black man and ending up as a white woman, what's that all about?"), crucial admissions ("I have devils inside that fight me. I'm my own worst enemy") and fascinating and insightful musical talk. It's a full chapter in Brown's book.

The resulting feature article, titled 'Found: Pop's Lost Genius', ran in England's *Daily Telegraph* magazine on 1 February 2003. The next night a chauffeured Spector hit the nightspots of LA; the following morning Lana Clarkson was dead from a single gunshot to the mouth, and the crime scene was Spector's castle. Brown, following the first details on the news, was able to recognise the rooms and furniture from his interview. The reconstruction of the murder and the days and months after slows the action of the book, to Spector's disadvantage. We learn much more about his habit of threatening women with guns, especially if they wished to leave his house at night. And we see in his aggressive posturing after Clarkson's death, both legally and in his public utterances ("she kissed the gun"), someone with no moral core.

In the end it's an old story: a great artist can be a nasty person. Whether Spector did it or not, his association with guns and his cracked personal behaviour were an accident waiting to happen. Brown, who has a limited background in writing music books – the first publication listed in his biography is *Richard Branson: An Inside Story* – does a fine job; he guides readers through the technicalities of the wall of sound and gives appropriate period music detail to denote 'feel'. His style is solid and entertaining, with no manufactured noir weirdness to mirror the life of his subject. Brown quotes from the famed Tom Wolfe portrait of Spector in 1965, 'The First Tycoon of Teen', and his sniffy description of some of it as "hyperbolic overdrive" shows the distance he wants to impose. This is the level-headed 2007 approach to the carnage and the art, and the drier English chronicling of them works well.

The one false note is the book's tabloid title. The rise and fall of Phil Spector has nothing to do with tearing down the wall of sound. The records he made between 1961 and '71 are going to stand for as long as people are able to enjoy good music. What is being torn down, or at the very least shaken, is Phil Spector himself, and as this book so aptly shows, it's a process that began a long time ago.

The Uncorking

Mark Seymour's *Thirteen Tonne Theory*

The best description of Hunters and Collectors' music, especially in their first incarnation, comes from their percussionist, Greg Perano, who when asked by a suspicious English customs officer to describe the band's sound replied, "Reggae-funk fusion with rock roots and a tinge of New York underground in the guitars." It is doubtful whether a customs officer anywhere in the world has ever heard such a confident and succinct summary of a group's music under the pressure of a border crossing, and it remains as good a grab as any at defining the band's sound and approach in its early years. The music got more commercial and straight-ahead as the group shifted its focus to the suburban-pub circuit and the record company called for hits. But from the start Hunters and Collectors had the talent and ambition to live up to these deftly stated influences, and although their inspiration may have thinned over the years, in the process a successful 18-year career was built – one that is now etched deep in Australian rock history.

Mark Seymour, the band's lead singer, guitarist and songwriter, is here to tell the story. And he does it very well. *Thirteen Tonne Theory: Life Inside Hunters and Collectors* (Penguin, 2008) is, in fact, a breakthrough rock biography, for not only has Seymour managed to get the band's history down in a fresh and entertaining manner, he has done it in an inventive way that leaves much rock history and memoir, here and overseas, looking stodgy and uninspired. Seymour has gone for the snapshot approach, small single-theme chapters that have the enigma and impact of short stories, and in doing so has skipped the bog of naming years and pinning down dates, and the whole weary 'and then we did this and then we did that' which strangles much middle-of-the-road biography. Instead, the chapters – mostly five to ten pages long – zoom in on pivotal or odd moments, giving the book the impressionistic air of good fiction while simultaneously allowing a surprisingly clear and detailed account of the group's history to emerge. Also, these fleeting shots of band life and decisive career moments help convey the heightened and often disjointed sense of things that can come from being in a famous rock band.

All of this smart jump-cut storytelling would be of little use if Seymour couldn't write, but he can. There are two surprises in this book. The first is that Seymour can craft sentence and paragraph, weave in dialogue and know when to gracefully exit a chapter. And the second is his authorial voice. This is the big surprise. For those who'd seen Mark Seymour as the bantam-sized, bulging T-shirted, ultra-serious lead singer hollering over his band, the tone of his book will come as a revelation. And perhaps it shouldn't. Perhaps Seymour was like this all along, known to his friends and fans as the warm, generous, laconic and, most importantly, self-deprecating person we meet in this book. But as the author himself admits, diplomacy and judgement have not always been his strengths. The book is littered with explosions or suppressed explosions and inner tension. Clarity may have come with the writing and the ten years that have passed since the break-up of his beloved band.

Wisely, he begins the story at Melbourne University, meeting future Hunters and Collectors bass player John Archer. Childhood is ditched. This is the first swerve away from the routine showbiz biography, and it is welcome. The book bursts into life in no less a way than Hunters and Collectors burst upon the Melbourne music scene of late 1980. They were an intriguing bunch of musicians, and the casting and formation of the band has a cinematic quality to it: handsome, swarthy young men in '30s suits on a mission. Scorsese would love it. The beginnings of the band were decidedly arty, and one of the few false notes in the book comes when Seymour states, "Whatever 'cool' was, we simply weren't it, and we never were over the entire 18 years." This is not true. The band was named after a Can song, they had Perano banging a hot-water cylinder on stage, Richard Lowenstein was making their videos, and they were soon signed to Virgin Records in London – the home of PiL, Magazine and XTC. This is cool; Seymour is right, though, to maintain that the cool did not last long. What brought its end was the convergence of two things: the failure of the band to break through in Europe on their first trip, and the need to survive artistically and financially in Australia. It led to a ditching of the art and the first hints of the move to the suburbs and regional towns.

Before this, Seymour fires off a few chapters on the band's rise, and none are funnier or more accurate than the two that chronicle the group's meetings with record companies. The first sees Mushroom Records head Michael Gudinski in full early-'80s form, stomping on his desk while offering a startled Hunters and Collectors not only a record deal but their own label. And the second is set in London with A&R guru Simon Draper of Virgin Records. This is a comic masterpiece of Australians in Pommie-land worthy of Barry Humphries, as the nine-piece band, two-man road crew and three girlfriends cram into a tiny Notting Hill office to be indulged (hash, champagne and £30,000) and then told exactly where and with whom they will be recording their next album. Unfortunately, the record-signing celebrations continue. At an Indian restaurant, an aggressively inebriated member of the entourage informs the all-powerful Mr Draper, "You see us as a bunch of colonials who'll just fuck it up ... you poncey little blue-blood. You just don't get us, do you? Do you?" With this, and more that came on the night, Hunters and Collectors died in Europe.

Seymour doesn't just leave the episode there; after hilariously and ruefully laying out the shenanigans and crimes of his band, the record company and the English in general, Seymour adds a postscript both bitter and perceptive. The chapter is called 'Virgin #3: Animal Farm'. It begins with the Orwell quote "All animals are equal, but some animals are more equal than others" and goes on to wring a startling admission out of the author. "The right thing to do next was that somebody, probably me, should have gone round to Draper's and humbly apologised. Instead, as always, the cork was pushed back in tightly. The band closed ranks and the problem wasn't addressed." And here's the heart of the book.

Seymour is obsessed with Hunters and Collectors. Other musicians have written about their bands, but it is difficult to think of anyone who has devoted so much effort to the internal wiring and mechanics of their own group. The band's successes and failures and career-hops all get chronicled, but it's the uniqueness of Hunters and Collectors – the all-consuming fire of their live show playing off against the anal-retentive, almost military nature of their organisation – that Seymour wants to examine. Where most groups are a casual coming together of social misfits, Hunters and Collectors was a business from the start, with rules, punishments for breaking them and an approach to work, ownership and shared creativity that was most un-rocklike. Seymour compares Hunters and Collectors to a trade union and to Trappist monks; a record producer called them "a bunch of communists". They were a large all-male group who approached the rock industry with suspicion and guile, and with the idea of building assets and attitude into a fortress, a position of self-contained power that would allow them to deal with the music business on the best possible terms. With all the associated themes of masculinity and democracy, it's an approach that appealed to Seymour. He signed onto it, and gave the copyrights to his songs to the group as he did so. It strangled him slowly, and the goodbye chapter to the band is free of tears.

Success did come and it doesn't make for dull reading. It is a very Australian situation, where the riches gained in this land have to be spent conquering others, and Hunters and Collectors tried like so many bands before. The attempts are mostly comical in Seymour's wry telling. Hunters and Collectors' suspicion of hype and trends was never going to be an advantage in cracking the very markets that subsist on the latest thing and flashy displays of charisma and image. Australia was the level playing field for the band, where triumphs could be built on road miles, an impressive PA and production, and the desire to kick arse live. It meant nothing to Dutch and Swedish rock journalists who taunted the hapless Seymour in interviews. So the second half of the book is the tale of two lands, the constant knocking on success's door with Midnight Oil leading the way through Europe and America, and then the return to the comforts and the wild shores of Australian rock 'n' roll – a place where audience members are known as punters, the veneration of the road crew and their eating habits exists, and the legendary Hunters and Collectors rider provokes a stunned Peter Garrett to exclaim, "They'll never drink that."

Thirteen Tonne Theory deserves to find a readership outside the rock community. Any Australian in any field of endeavour, whether within the arts or out in rougher terrain, would be proud to have written a memoir as good as this. Many novelists are not going to get close when they look back. Seymour has cracked it open with sliced-up chapters, an enigmatic approach to time, and his ability to lace a cocky and colloquial manner with vulnerability and wit. Anyone who comes after him to write of their years and careers in rock music must know that this is the book they are going to have to trump.

The 5000 Spirits or The Layers of the Onion

Joe Boyd's *White Bicycles: Making Music in the 1960s*

A friend of mine, younger than I, who works for a hip reissue label out of San Francisco, told me of an encounter with a member of a prominent San Franciscan band of the '60s. My friend, aided perhaps by the fact that he is not a native of the city, enjoys good relations with and access to most of the band members and scenesters of this time. He's done many formal interviews, and has strong connections with them through his work and his passion as a fan. The interview with this particular band member was frosty and stiff from the start, my friend's enthusiasm brought to a swift close (after one too many questions about life in Haight-Ashbury) with a dismissive, "Man, you're just one of those people who just weren't there."

Memoirs of the '60s can be a bit like that, and to be fair it must be hard to keep that tone out of any recollection of a decade so tumultuous, blasted and candy-coloured. But it does creep in, and for those of us enthralled by the era and especially its music, it can be a little bit galling to hear, yet again, that true understanding comes only to those with Woodstock tickets still in their back pockets. No such problem with Joe Boyd, though, who was at Woodstock and yet has written a lucid, clear-eyed account of his life during the '60s, light on the Man-you-should-have-been-theres and full of good, elegant prose.

So who's Joe Boyd? If you have an early Fairport Convention album, or either of the first two Nick Drake albums, or know the first Pink Floyd single 'Arnold Layne', or have boogied to Maria Muldaur's AM hit 'Midnight at the Oasis', then you know Joe Boyd already. He produced them. But there's more to his story than late-night studio tales, and that's what makes *White Bicycles* (Serpent's Tail, 2006) such a breathtaking read.

We've come to see and know a lot of the '60s through rock-star and rock-mogul and rock-groupie biographies, and many of them have the protagonist famous and well kitted-out by '66. But that's when Boyd gets his first record-producer jobs; before that there's a story that has your head shaking, as the Zelig-like Boyd bounces through the early '60s from the US to England to Europe, seemingly fitted with some radar device that's going to drop him into the hottest music scene going.

Boyd's book is subtitled 'Making Music in the 1960s', and from its enigmatic opening line – "The sixties began in the summer of 1956, ended in October of 1973 and peaked just before dawn on 1 July 1967 during a set by Tomorrow at the UFO Club in London" – that's what you get. No childhood moments. No leafy Boston reminiscences. Not even his parents' first names. The book leaps straight into the music, with the author at age 12 hooked on doo-wop and early R&B on *American Bandstand*. The next jump is to Harvard in 1960, where Boyd is listening to the blues. How he got into this university and what he studied there is never revealed. He graduated in early '64 and in any other decade would have gone into a cosy professional niche for life, but this is the '60s, so his first job is tour-managing Muddy Waters.

This is where the fun begins. Boyd lives a charmed life, a music aficionado's dream. Being from Boston means instant immersion in that city's incredible folk scene; it also puts him in a proto-'60s environment of bells, Zen texts, marijuana, visits to Mexico, and strummin' guitars that are going to ride out the decade. The local music is Joan Baez, Eric Von Schmidt, Jim Kweskin and the Jug Band (Maria Muldaur on lead vocals) and informal visits from Bob Dylan, up from New York. It's a swirling world, with Boyd – at this point barely more than 20 – hustling as concert promoter for old blues legends Lonnie Johnson and Sleepy

John Estes, while trying to manoeuvre himself onto the budding Elektra recording label as an A&R man *and* working as both booking agent and dogsbody for the Newport jazz and folk festivals. Talk about being at the centre of things.

Over the next two years, with these jobs in place, Boyd meets a fantastic array of eccentrics and the soon-to-be-famous. Here, the radar comes out: he helps put together The Lovin' Spoonful in New York, then goes to Chicago and discovers The Paul Butterfield Blues Band, then travels through northern England and Scotland seeing the English folk revival whose flowering he'll record in a few years, then heads into London to record a pre-Cream Eric Clapton and Jack Bruce on 'Crossroads'. And this is just a snippet.

Meanwhile, he's tour managing jazz giants Coleman Hawkins, Roland Kirk, Stan Getz and the divine Astrid Gilberto through Europe. But there's no money, and the big names and breaks are tempered by Boyd's frustration at not being able to capitalise on his discoveries. Between '64 and '66 everyone is positioning, no one more so than Dylan and his manager, Albert Grossman, who decide to play out one the great dramas of the decade at the '65 Newport Folk Festival. And this is where the tempo of the book slows and settles, as Boyd lays out beautifully the events of that epic weekend with the ultimate insider's view.

The '65 Newport Folk Festival is a tragi-comedy of such a size, populated with characters of so sharp a definition, that it is amazing no one has put it up for a film. In short, Dylan goes electric: backed by The Paul Butterfield Blues Band, a screaming Mike Bloomfield on lead guitar, he leads the charge with three electric numbers that splinter the cosy mid-'60s folk community. Around this performance spin all the factions, some wishing to cut the electric cables and kill the sound, others dancing, others claiming Dylan is crying on stage. And who is at the mixing desk, who set up the amplifiers, who runs back to the desk with orders from folk veteran Pete Seeger to turn it down? Joe Boyd. It's a great chapter.

Boyd's main legacy as a producer is a brace of albums that he made in London between '66 and '70. The groups and singers bear exotic names: Fairport Convention, The Incredible String Band, Fotheringay, Nick Drake. Their music is the exhaustion that was inevitable at the end of a gruelling decade of trends and movements. It's hippie folk, but it's the very best of it and it has aged well. Boyd found his home here, the American with the exquisite folk-rock credentials meeting a group of talented English and Scottish songwriters and musicians schooled on the same roots. But they bring a twist, a particular Britishness to it all: with Fairport it was the first great electrification of English folk music, for Nick Drake it was Keats and Coleridge, and for The Incredible String Band it was the whole '60s caravan.

The ten best albums from this period live on. And it's to Boyd's credit that he fostered these talents and recorded them so well. He has remained a custodian to them, and seen their currency in the rock world rise. Nick Drake, especially, has come in for a major re-evaluation; revered in his day by insiders, his hushed dark-wood folk sounds spectacular now. Homage has also come from the freak-folk scene, a new wave of bands and singers who take inspiration from these records, and who all look suspiciously like The Incredible String Band circa '68.

But the dream had to die. This was not an age of brand-naming the band and building the franchise; more a situation in wild flux, with talented people exploding around drugs, relationships and the ideals that they packed into their music. Boyd is overworked and, struggling with budgets and record-company problems, watches his world fall apart and begins to contemplate his future. Sandy Denny leaves Fairport, Nick Drake slips further into the depression that will lead to his death in '74, The Incredible String Band finds Scientology. Boyd takes a chance in LA.

A little heat goes out of the book here. It's as if, after the glories of Boston and London, LA is a step too far. As the new head of the music department for Warner Brothers Film, Boyd arrives expecting to install mavericks such as John Cale in the system. He soon learns the lessons of dollars and sense. His first jobs, working on the soundtracks of *A Clockwork Orange* and *Deliverance*, proved disappointments: creative input was denied. Both films are dealt with in a page of *White Bicycles*. Boyd had left his fiefdom in London and walked straight into American corporate culture, carrying a naivety and a bag of ideas that had got him through the '60s – but the '60s were no more.

The overwhelming virtue of this book is the level of its gaze. It's a magic-carpet ride of the highs and lows, and not one locked into one career on one trip. Boyd fulfils his dream of becoming a record producer, but even at the moment of realisation he's putting on the first London gigs for Pink Floyd. And it's that scope of experience, the interconnections and the skill with which they are woven into the narrative, that make this book a cut above so many others about the era.

The story also benefits from Boyd himself, a most unlikely '60s figure in a way; more the white-suited explorer of old, who finds himself not in Africa but wandering in the jungles of that mad decade. Somebody had to make sense of it then; somebody has to make sense of it now. Who better than Joe Boyd?

Rock and Roll Babble On

Nick Kent's *Apathy for the Devil: A 1970s Memoir*

To read the *New Musical Express (NME)* in the '70s was one of the great joys of the decade. It was an insider's choice and the seriousness of any new acquaintance's enthusiasm for music could be instantly gauged by whether they read it or not. The readership of the London-based weekly was predominantly male and in the 15-to-30 age bracket, and many a school project or office job was delayed subject to the lure of the latest Roxy Music review or the inside story of the current Led Zeppelin tour. At the forefront of the paper were its three greatest writers: Ian MacDonald, Charles Shaar Murray and Nick Kent. They had been taken on in 1972, when the paper was given just 12 weeks to reverse years of falling circulation. All three were recruited from the embers of the late-'60s countercultural London street press and came with a belief that rock music, the British scene especially, warranted a tougher and smarter level of rock criticism. MacDonald wrote with great authority and tended to concentrate on progressive groups and '60s artists. Murray, in contrast, had a very engaging, almost slang-like style, and raced from blues bands to The Ramones to Bowie. And Nick Kent? Well, every cliché about rock writers as rock stars begins with him; his prose rambled freely from the overblown to the succinct and powerful, and he had a musical aesthetic second to none. In fact, you could say he helped invent punk rock.

Apathy for the Devil is his second book since leaving the *NME* in the early '80s. He has not been prolific, nor has he prospered in a second career. His problem has been drugs: heavy heroin use from 1974 to '78, methadone until the late '80s, plus assorted other "chemicals" – to pick up Kent-speak – such as cocaine, amphetamines, valium and marijuana.

His music journalism over the last decades has been infrequent, with no body of work to match his glory years at the *NME* in the '70s. He has become a legend, both for his writing, which was always handwritten and submitted at the last minute, and for the larger-than-life, or larger-than-print, persona he generated through his prose. His memoir deals in the collusion between music and drugs – how the belief in either can lead to the need of the other, and how the belief in both can only lead to disaster. *Apathy* mirrors the quandary, and although Kent brings in many theories and factors to dissect the music of the '70s, the good and bad of the decade, the good and bad of the book, lies at the fault-line where heroin takes over his life.

He was born in London in 1951, the only child of loving middle-class parents. His father was a sound engineer, his mother a schoolteacher – books and music (Beethoven, Wagner, Debussy, Ravel) were in the house. By the early '60s the generation gap was opening up and what really had the steam coming out of his father's ears was pop music. Kent was entranced, and in a life-changing episode he not only witnessed the Rolling Stones in concert in 1964, but got to visit the band backstage. Bill and Charlie are towelling down, Keith is almost asleep on a sofa, Jagger is scowling and moody and Brian Jones has three women around him and is perfectly charming; for the bug-eyed 13-year-old, the die is cast: "I was smitten ... suddenly I had my future adult agenda mapped out before me."

The late '60s and very early '70s are beautifully evoked in the early chapters, as the hippie dream hardens around London squat life. A fair swathe of prime psychedelia is witnessed, including what Kent still regards as the best bill of his life: The Jimi Hendrix Experience, Syd Barrett-era Pink Floyd, The Move and The Nice. An interest in literature dictates his choice of university, Bedford College in Regent's Park, where Kent joins two other male students in a dormitory with 23 women under the spell of *Tea for the Tillerman*-era Cat Stevens. His virginity is lost here. Kent gains a post as music critic for *Frendz* magazine and the *NME* calls soon after. The book swirls at this moment, as Kent lays out a set of influences on his writing while chronicling with great enthusiasm a series of vital gigs that not only sharpen his musical vision but will reverberate down the decade as a trail of fire he will lay to the start of punk. The literary influences are not too surprising: new journalism titans Capote and Wolfe are mentioned, and also their disciples working in the American rock press, such as Hunter S Thompson and Lester Bangs at *Rolling Stone* and *Creem* – both magazines at their height in '71, and forerunners to the *NME* reign of supremacy. The shows Kent sees in quick succession in 1971–72 are the London debuts of the MC5, Iggy and the Stooges, Lou Reed, Can, Captain Beefheart and the Magic Band, plus Bowie's first Ziggy Stardust show. This is the future of rock for Kent and he has a readership of 100,000 (and growing) to tell it to.

At heart he is romantic; in music, women (bohemian and French) and drugs, and his writing has always appealed to rock 'n' roll romantics. No synthesisers, chin-stroking progressive rock or soppy singer–songwriters for Nick Kent. He called his first book, which was mostly a collection of his rock journalism, *The Dark Stuff*, and that is what has always drawn him. At times, even back in the '70s, it made him look ridiculous, but his strike rate as a critic was always high.

He wrote a stunning re-appraisal of Neil Young's *On the Beach* after its widespread damnation on release as "depressing" and a waste of Young's talent. Long pieces on Syd Barrett and Nick Drake resurrected artists who had quickly fallen from the public eye. A two-page report from New York in early '76 alerted most of the world to the existence of The Ramones, Talking Heads and Blondie. Morrissey wrote to him incessantly as a teenager, and Chrissie Hynde of The Pretenders left her hometown of Akron, Ohio, to come to London on the strength of a Kent piece about her beloved Iggy and the Stooges.

The first half of the book marches along well; there is focus and fire as we get the career-ascending years from the "Zeitgeist-surfing dark prince of seventies rock journalism", as he proudly or ironically (hard to tell) calls himself in the first sentence of the third chapter. The book cracks badly, though, midway, and without wishing to push the correlation between drug abuse and talent abuse too hard, the two meet here – to be precise, at an after-show party for Rod Stewart and the Faces at Cher's home in Los Angeles in 1975. Kent, displaying a typically perverse sense of logic and location, had come to LA to get off drugs and it is during a long, wearisome description of the après-gig celebration seen through a drug haze that the book turns. Kent the truth-teller becomes Kent the rock 'n' roll-Babylon bore, a transformation capped by two absurd stories. The first, involving guitarist Dickey Betts of The Allman Brothers Band (who isn't even at the party), has Betts riding on his Harley and spying a bull in a field, killing it with his bare hands, and then cooking and eating it by the roadside. "Clearly these were fellows not to trifle with," warns Kent, and presumably they had barbecues on the back of their Harleys too. The second backroom story has the rotund manager of Led Zeppelin, Peter Grant, inadvertently sitting on Elvis Presley's father. Even Kent doubts the veracity of this one, "but that doesn't stop me from wanting to believe it's true". On such a premise anything could be put into a book.

Apathy does have a villain and it's clothes-shop owner and Sex Pistols manager Malcolm McLaren. He's welcome in any memoir as he gives good quote, is full of crazy ideas and, as Kent admits, got things done because he was one of the few people in the decade *not* on drugs. The episodes that heavily involve him appear after the LA sojourn and pull the book back into stride for a time. That Kent was in the Sex Pistols is the big secret of the memoir for those who don't know his '70s journalism. It was for only two months in the middle of '75, as McLaren madly shuffled to get the ultimate line-up of the band in place. Kent, who was on guitar, is fired. Steve Jones, who was the singer, becomes the guitarist, and then Johnny Rotten is discovered in McLaren's shop. It is a supreme serendipity that the man who has been shepherding punk into print for the previous three years finds himself, albeit briefly, in the breakthrough band. It places him exquisitely to chronicle punk when it takes off in the following year, but Kent has scars, some very real, as from a chain-beating inflicted by Sid Vicious supposedly at McLaren's behest, and others harder to quantify, involving Kent's continual homeless existence and his full-blown drug use. Both these conditions lead him to form an odd relationship with his attacker, Vicious, and his American girlfriend Nancy Spungen; and so, as London simmers under its greatest musical and cultural surge since psychedelia, Kent tells the tale of Sid and Nancy while pouring invective on the "puppet-master" McLaren.

To read Nick Kent in the '70s was exhilarating. There were the famous long pieces, there were the defining acts at the heart of his world: Dylan/The Velvet Underground/The Rolling Stones/Iggy Pop – the dark stuff. And importantly, though not so prominently in *Apathy for the Devil*, there was Kent's perspective on newer artists. When he praised acts such as The Only Ones, The Cramps, Jonathan Richman and the Modern Lovers or the early Pretenders, people went out and bought their records. An amazing rave on Television's *Marquee Moon* was enough to land the album in the British Top 30. Bizarrely Kent overlooks this side of his work, too busy gruffly tearing at his enemies or writing vapid page-long summaries of 'name' artists that could be pulled from any rock almanac and then spicing them with a little insider gossip. Kent has managed the improbable: he has written himself out of the decade he helped to shape.

CONCERTS

Soft Touch

Nana Mouskouri

In a far corner of my mind there has always been a place for Nana Mouskouri. She resides there with a few others: Marcel Marceau, Charles Aznavour, Juliette Gréco. Post-war bohemians. Café performers who got onto TV or into the concert halls early, who had a few hits or breakthrough shows, who managed to expand it into a European career and then tour the rest of the world, usually to the outposts of their own community. But the sun is going down. Marceau and Aznavour are in their eighties, Gréco in her seventies. How old is Roger Whittaker? James Last is doing techno in Germany. And Nana has decided to call it a day.

It's funny how we allot certain people places in our imagination, and then over the years, as each new morsel of information comes in, we add it to the list we have of the person, never perhaps making a full picture, but gathering facts here and there that round the person out a little in our minds. In 1962 Nana made an album in New York called *The Girl from Greece Sings*, produced by heavy-duty soul and R&B ace Quincy Jones. Early in her career she sang Bob Dylan songs. And then in 1969 she went to a concert at the invitation of Leonard Cohen, who had also asked Dylan along. Dylan asked her who her favourite singer was. She answered Oum Kalthoum. Dylan was stunned; she was his too. Small morsels, but they added to the portrait.

Nana's genius is that she has never changed. To the broadest edges of show business, change is encouraged. Madonna and Kylie Minogue live and die by it. Nana still has the jet-black shoulder-length hair. The black-rimmed glasses. And the faint smile. Contempt? World-weariness? Who knows? But it's been there, staring out from her concert ads in metropolitan newspapers, for as long as I can remember. It was there again in June when her last ever tour of Australia was announced.

I'd see her on German TV variety shows in the 1990s and she always exuded great mystery. There was either some kind of intellect or artistic intent behind her, or nothing at all. Given the Dylan covers, the choice of Oum Kalthoum and the connection with Cohen, I thought there had to be something. Plus I dug the curtain of black hair, the glasses, the almost medicated impassiveness of everything she did.

Now I'm in seat T32 of the Sydney Opera House – 20 rows back and she looks fantastic. Before her entrance we were shown a five-minute film of her career. There was lots of great '60s and '70s footage, and then a cut to Nana on the streets of Kenya in the late '90s drew a gasp from the audience. She looked fuller in the face, and older. The shock of seeing this up against the sculpted ancient footage had momentarily set up a what-are-we-going-to-see-here scenario. But there she is, in sparkling white, hair black, high heels, trim. The remarkable Nana.

And then bang, she goes straight into Dylan's 'I'll Remember You'. It's her first message to us on a night of farewells. The show is split in two: the first part is more experimental and roaming, and in the second half come the show-stoppers. Strangely, for someone who has sung so much, her voice gets better and stronger as the show goes on. 'The First Time Ever I Saw Your Face' is followed by a wonderful version of 'Scarborough Fair'. Her tactic is to drain the songs of a little of their sensuality and to interpret them for their melodies. She uses her voice as an instrument, treating the songs the way a great instrumentalist would, coasting on the melody and joyfully exposing the craft and beauty of the notes. She switches to a warmer, more lilting tone, for a brace of Greek folk songs. And then comes Dylan's 'A Hard Rain's a-Gonna Fall', in

French, not some truncated version but the whole four verses, six minutes long, with the band on full throttle, Nana's arms flailing in the air. It brings the night alive and sends us out to the foyer, buzzing.

The crowd is European, with hardly an Aussie accent to be heard. There are people in their late fifties to seventies, well dressed, with gold chains on handbags and coiffured, luxuriant hair. Their children are here too, brought up on Nana, sons in their twenties who have come with their mothers.

Then she's back, this time in red, and with her six-piece band once again. The pick of them is the drummer, who adds some much-appreciated drive to the proceedings. But no one ever encroaches, no one goes off the leash. This is Nana's show. It's restrained; nothing really catches fire. This is smooth, studied professionalism, one show on a world tour that has been rehearsed to within an inch of its life. Except that right in the centre rests the one point of uncertainty, of hesitancy: Nana herself.

There are two wonders of the show. The first is this sense of vulnerability she projects. In an age of sock-it-to-'em show business – think Bette Midler, Barbra Streisand – it's a pleasure to hear and watch a performer hold back and perform within herself. Maybe it's a European trait, but it is so appealing to see someone so talented and secure in their gift who has no desire to pummel or annihilate the people that pay to see her. And this is why they love her – she has a soft touch.

The second wonder is her artistry. Her band's restraint gives her the room to soar. Her repertoire swings from movie themes to '60s singer–songwriters to Broadway and beyond. She's middle of the road but all over the road; in lesser hands it would make for a wild mix. Yet everything she sings has gravity, no matter how far she strays into kitsch, and she can stray a long way. The songs anchor her. Her cool, crystal voice pulls her through, bringing new meaning to songs you have heard many times before.

The second half of the show is the career highlights. She talks more – this is, after all, her farewell, and she wants to impart her life and her music one last meaningful time. So she sings 'Somewhere Over the Rainbow' (her father was a movie projectionist) and then a stunning, jazzy 'Autumn Leaves'. Her big ballads – 'Bridge Over Troubled Water', 'The Rose', Joni Mitchell's 'Both Sides Now' – capture the youthful bohemianism of the audience's past. She loves the '60s singer–songwriters and it is uplifting to hear a genuine '60s spirit breathe life into them. In a far-off galaxy, Nana Mouskouri may be the outermost edge of folk rock.

She leaves in triumph. No tears. A wave. An armful of red roses. Good on her for leaving now. This isn't Cher on a battleship or being lowered from the ceiling in a cage. This is a 70-year-old Greek woman getting out of show business; a very fine voice, wrapped in artistic temperament, slipping out into the night.

Tales from Pig City

The Saints

Pig City isn't a nice name for a town, is it? When Unkle Fats and the Parameters released a single in 1986 called 'Pig City', the meaning of its title was immediately clear. 'Pig' meant police and 'city' was the town where the band lived, which was Brisbane. When the local music journalist Andrew Stafford released a book in 2004 on the history of the town's music scene and its related cultural forces, he named it *Pig City: From The Saints to Savage Garden*. And now comes Pig City the Musical! Well, not exactly a musical, but a big day of bands under a circus tent to kick off the Queensland Music Festival, and in the coup to end all coups, the headline act of the day, hitting the stage at 8.40 pm, is The Saints.

Not The Saints that lead singer Chris Bailey has been fronting for years, but a line-up that includes original guitarist Ed Kuepper and original drummer Ivor Hay. The stakes are upped considerably. This is a reunion that doesn't have the feel of inevitability about it. And for all the publicity and drawing power of the other bands on the bill, covering the Brisbane scene over the past three decades, without The Saints there'd be perhaps 1000 people here; with The Saints it's full at 7000 and has the sort of buzz which means, no matter what happens during the day, that the night is going to end with a massive cherry on top. For this formation of the band hasn't played together for almost 30 years, and when they walk on stage – Bailey and Kuepper from opposite sides, as it turns out – they are going to put the whole legacy on the line, in a one-off gig in front of a home-town crowd.

Punk hit Brisbane like no other city in Australia. The tentacles that grew out of New York and London from the musical explosion of 1976 affected the receptive waiting enclaves in each major city around the globe in varying ways. As the music and images of the Ramones, Patti Smith, early Pere Ubu, Television and the Sex Pistols were heard and seen, bands formed, systems started and the word spread. Brisbane was different, for two main reasons: we had Bjelke-Petersen and The Saints. Bjelke-Petersen represented the kind of crypto-fascist, bird-brained conservatism that every punk lead singer in the world could only dream of railing against. His use of a blatantly corrupt police force, and its heavy-handed response to punk, gave the scene a political edge largely absent in the other states. And The Saints were the musical revolutionaries in the city's evil heart.

The Saints, as far back as 1973–74, were joining the dots of the coming revolution. History gets hazy here, and a little contentious in trying to place the band in the queue of punk's forerunners. But in 1976, with the release of the almighty '(I'm) Stranded' single, the band landed early and with a considerable thump. They left Brisbane soon after, having stayed long enough to record their debut album, before leapfrogging Sydney and Melbourne to London, where they recorded their second and third albums. That became the total catalogue of the first, and clearly best, line-up of the band. The fact that they came from Brisbane, and thus gave a city that usually chased music history a place *in* history, was not lost on the following generations of bands or the city's cultural arbiters. It also meant, as is often the case with famous artists from provincial cities, that the relationship the artists have with the city is prickly, old scores are not forgotten as the city struggles to accommodate the artists' burgeoning myth, and this is certainly the case with The Saints.

At the centre of the band is the relationship between Chris Bailey and Ed Kuepper. In terms of intriguing rock couples, this one is a beauty.

In Brisbane there is a legion of observers of the friendship; sub-branches exist in Sydney and London. Every move one of them makes in relation to the other, every crack they have at each other in the press, every sleeve or thank-you list in album reissues from the past 30 years, gets analysed and turned over. The rumour mill about both of them is ridiculous. In the days before the Pig City show the word is that they're not talking to each other, that they're having the time of their lives, that Kuepper's fed up and vowing never to do it again, that they're spotted laughing together in a pub; Bailey's mad, Kuepper's angry, Kuepper's mad, Bailey's angry. I have two days of people giving me breathless and completely contradictory accounts of what's happening. In the end it's so confusing, and the changes in people's perceptions so regular, that it's hard not to believe Bailey and Kuepper are orchestrating the whole thing themselves, and then phoning each other late at night to chuckle over the mayhem and hyper-analysis that follows in their wake.

But the differences between them are real: the acrimonious split-up of the original band back in 1978, Chris Bailey's use of The Saints' name without Kuepper (or Hay) and the clear fork of their solo careers show two artists at variance with one another. Teenage years may have thrown them together but their moves since 1978, the music they have made apart, would not lead you to believe that they were once in the same band. The points of divergence between them can be chased down a number of routes. First, there's the clear personality difference. Bailey is the showman on and off stage, flamboyant and gregarious: the Irishman with his poetry, soul and wine in tow. Kuepper is intense and inward, of German extraction: he is the technician with his eye always on the music. There is also the division between Bailey's more mainstream take on rock, soul and folk, and Kuepper's far more eclectic journey through jazz, country and on to noise. From 1973 to '78, though, they worked brilliantly together; it got them out of Brisbane, and left three albums that stand up extremely well against much of the post-'76 punk-rock deluge.

What happened between them is that they complemented each other. Kuepper's songwriting magnificently served Bailey's voice, while Bailey got to sing and provide lyrics to melodies better than he could write. The personalities were a natural play-off, too: Bailey the charismatic lead singer; Kuepper hunched over his guitar, feeding Bailey the confidence to take his frontman persona as far as he wanted to take it. And for the audience there was the sheer joy of seeing two very different guys, each with his own strong points, go into some kind of jigsaw lock that instantly produced fully formed and powerful music.

The first song they play at the Pig City show is 'Swing for the Crime', off *Prehistoric Sounds*, their third and best album, and straight away you know it's going to be a great night. Ivor Hay is pounding the jungle beat, Caspar Wijnberg is solid on bass, but all eyes are on Kuepper and Bailey. The former is in front of two Marshall stacks. He might not be playing the red Gibson SG from the '70s to satisfy the obsessives, but the sound is instantly recognisable. Kuepper is not going to cut corners; this is the original guitar sound resurrected, and it's massive. Bailey – thin, rat-haired, in a black suit and white top – is the consummate rock frontman. But the first ten minutes spin by in a daze. I'm almost lost in just realising that this reunion, always thought highly improbable, is happening. That's the first feeling. The second is how bloody good they are.

You can see the chemistry immediately: Chris Bailey and Ed Kuepper make one of the best partnerships in Australian rock, or rock 'n' roll anywhere. Which is not to forget the role of Ivor Hay. He is vital, not only because of his inventive drumming but also because of the authority he holds over Kuepper and Bailey, both of whom turn to him regularly through the performance: Kuepper for rhythmic sustenance and to wind down the endings of songs; Bailey to find an encouraging grin every time he turns to the drum riser. The genial Hay, who has spent the past 16 years away from the music business, also has a role as a useful third party to the machinations of the Kuepper–Bailey partnership.

The set is a dream run through the band's early catalogue. Helped by a brass section that trots on and off the stage, the songs visit two camps. There are the big, driving ballads from *Prehistoric Sounds*: 'Chameleon', 'The Prisoner' and 'All Times Through Paradise'. And there are the very best of the short, sharp tunes scattered across the first two albums: '(I'm) Stranded', 'No Time', 'Know Your Product' and 'This Perfect Day'. The total effect is unrelenting quality and depth of vision. This is no punk ram-a-lam, but a full showing of the original breadth and beauty The Saints were able to put out in an era and in a town (London) which demanded that punk bands play by punk rules. The Saints' wilful bucking of the trends then allows the music to storm now. There is wonder here, and the brass section, with its stabs and swing, is no 'soul music' affectation or quote; it is welded into the rock form like few other bands have ever managed.

Chris Bailey's been waiting for this, no matter how much he might deny it or be blasé about it. Thousands of people in a tent in his home town is what he's been dreaming about. And we get it all. He flounces; he pirouettes; he speaks absolute gibberish between songs that somehow makes sense if you're in on the cosmic joke. Every rock-star gesture is down pat – the cigarette held elegantly in hand, the sweeping back of the long hair, the occasional jog from one side of the stage to the other – and not for one minute does it seem forced or have the feel of cliché about it. It's because he is both an original and a master of the lead-singer pose. Lesser mortals in front of big, brooding rock bands fall down on this stuff; Bailey strides with no hesitation, willing to take it to the limit. And if for a second he stumbles and looks the fool, then there's that voice. It's lost some of its phlegmy sneer from the '70s and now has a higher-pitched, stadium-rock veneer to it; if anything, and he was a great vocalist the first time around, he's got better. His singing is the revelation of the night. Kuepper's guitar playing, and the fine brace of songs they have, were known. But Bailey's singing – its presence, its soul – stuns.

And then there's Ed Kuepper. It's a pleasure to watch him wrestle the catalogue. If Bailey can at times seem a little cavalier with The Saints' legacy – though at this gig he is not – Kuepper is taking the opportunity to lay down the law on the way these songs were played originally and should be played henceforth. It's a master class in electric-guitar playing which has you realising that he's one of the very few Australian guitar geniuses. Obvious comparisons are with Neil Young or Kurt Cobain, sonic adventurers who can take sheets of electric noise and get songs out of them, while also being able to solo a hurricane of notes that mean something to the song. The force of Kuepper is such that he commands half the stage. It's a wall of sound and intensity, and it's telling that Bailey only enters Kuepper's side of the stage when he is at the peak of his rock-star game. When Bailey goes into one of his pre-song raves, such as the mock-Elizabethan one he did before the band hurled itself into '(I'm) Stranded' ("His hair it was longeth, and it groweth"), Kuepper grins, and it's not from embarrassment. You get the feeling he likes this side of Bailey: this antagonistic, no-holds-barred gonzo frontman who is just as out-there and in-your-face as Kuepper is with his guitar. Kuepper can sing and lead a band, but not like Bailey. And like all great duos, they pump each other up; when The Saints are on, it takes a place this size to hold the charisma and magic.

The Pig City performance was a triumph and, without wishing to besmirch any of the performers that came before them, The Saints strode the stage like giants. This is a band that still breathes fire. If they do no more, ever, then this one-off show has burnished the myth rather than tarnished it. More shows in the future, or a tour, would be most welcome, and if the rebirth of The Saints as a live band turned out to have occurred in Brisbane, it would be a lovely touch. And finally, if there is recording to be done with this line-up, then, based on the sparks on display, an album to join the glory of the first three would not be beyond them.

The *Countdown* Spectacular

Molly is up in the bleachers with a microphone and a spotlight on him. He's up there to introduce the last act of the night, Sherbet. He does it like this: he tells a woman at the end of an aisle that the band has missed its flight and won't be performing. He then goes to the man behind her and asks if he's a Broncos fan. One can only wonder what the waiting band thinks of this. Molly has been sent up there to 'vibe' the crowd but, though charming, he lost the ability to talk to anyone normal years ago. Finally, he reels back and shouts, "Sherbet!" Our eyes swing to the stage, where Daryl Braithwaite is standing amid his band, giggling. It's an endearing moment: no 'Christ on the cross' pose signalling a triumphant return, or sitting astride a strobe light; just a shy, nervous grin. A woman in front of me yells out, "I love you, Daryl!" The band crashes into 'Summer Love'.

'Spectacular' is the wrong word for this show. *Countdown* could never really be a spectacular, because it wasn't one to begin with. It was a TV show on a box, and that provides the contours of this show. No single act comes on and breathes fire into the corners of the arena and no one blows this up to anything bigger than what it is: a surprisingly entertaining, quick-shot run-through of singers, groups and their hit songs. A show relatively low on production values (the pyrotechnics must have cost all of $500), but high on guts and cheeky Australian charm.

The format helps. This is the first show I've ever seen like this, and it's a pleasure to know that no matter how bad someone is, you only have four minutes of them. One Swanee number is enough. That's no cheap-shot criticism – you hear his gut-scraping voice, know he's Jimmy Barnes's brother, hear Bon Scott in him, think about those connections, and then he's gone. Cheetah, two magnificently preserved women in their late forties, both the very definition of 'rock chick', glide across the stage to their hit 'Spend the Night', and that works too. Then there are The Choirboys, unknown to me, purveyors of some diabolical '80s rock, probably, but one admires the nifty three-chord dynamics of 'Run to Paradise'. An hour of them could be deadly, but extract the nugget, light them and give them a good PA, and it has you wishing more rock shows were like this: fast-paced, hits coming at you and everyone playing for their lives.

The show is split in two. The first half leans to the one-hit wonders; the second half more to the 'artists', who get two or three songs each. The first half is zanier: Frankie J Holden and Wilber Wilde from Ol' 55 are genuinely funny. And then come the Melbourne boys. There is a certain kind of pop star from this town, enthralled by David Bowie, who has never been able to divorce pop stardom from glitter. The trashy, high-camp aspects of *Countdown* suit them beautifully. They are living out dreams, and the eyeliner and hair dye have come out for the occasion. Brian Mannix (Uncanny X-Men), Dave Sterry from Real Life (a great 'Send Me an Angel') and Billy Miller from The Ferrets represent this contingent, and all are in their pomp.

The first half closes with Hush, and they are astonishing. They do 'Boney Maronie' and 'Glad All Over' and provide the one bug-eyed, I-can't-believe-what's-in-front-of-me moment of the night. This is a band that has gone through some life changes and come out the other side looking more interesting than they did in the '70s. Lead singer Keith Lamb, once the ultimate poodle-haired pop star, now looks like the kind of guy you see wandering through the Byron Bay markets: dreadlocks, weird clothes. Lead guitarist Les Gock is perma-cool, still wearing a guitar on his skinny frame like no one else in Oz rock ever has. They're on fire, a mad mash of heavy glam rock and someone who looks like John Butler's dad on vocals. Their next gig should be the Big Day Out.

The spoiler in all of this is a dance troupe that comes on in each half of the show to do routines from musicals and clips of the era. It doesn't work. Rock 'n' roll and pop (which is what this show aspires to) and dance troupes doing 'Footloose' don't mix. It immediately sends the rock 'n' roll to cabaret land, and it's the first time that I feel a twinge of embarrassment at being here.

Is Ross Wilson a genius? We're in the second half of the show and this question keeps coming back to me during the ten minutes or so that Mondo Rock is on stage. He's the one performer tonight whom you look at and think, He could have done something overseas if he'd wanted to. Everything about him is unique. The way he moves, dresses, sings – and his songs. Sure, Mondo Rock may not have been the most sympathetic vehicle, but it shows that in his third decade in the business he is still savvy and talented enough to have hits. The great 'Cool World' is the first one played tonight.

The show benefits from a strong dash of Melbourne music. Renée Geyer, Stephen Cummings, Joe Camilleri, The Models and James Reyne all lend credibility, and all come out in good spirits to revisit their moment(s) in the *Countdown* sun. Reyne is smart enough to strip the gorgeous 'Reckless' down to an acoustic guitar. Cummings blurts out 'Who Listens to the Radio?'. Then a certain gravitas comes to the night's proceedings with the arrival of Geyer. It's as if the crowd draws breath and settles to welcome a 'real' singer – a weird echo of the class she brought to '70s *Countdown*. She judges the mood just right, showing her vocal chops are still intact with 'It's a Man's World' and then letting go with a campy 'Say You Love Me'.

The Models are fun, too. They do two good songs, 'I Hear Motion' and 'Out of Mind, Out of Sight', plus there's the added pleasure of trying to gauge the current state of Sean Kelly and James Freud's friendship. Two songwriters and frontmen in a pop group is always a difficult ship to navigate, especially through the hit-single world. Judging from the distance between their microphones, one senses there's a certain tension between them still. But they need each other: Freud without Kelly is too cheesy; Kelly without Freud is too intense. One hopes they continue.

And then comes Leo Sayer. He's the performer I'd been dreading, and this is when the night turns – or, perhaps, some magic appears. Sayer comes on and is actually good. He fits. He makes the consummate entrance, touching every corner of the stage without for a second seeming to rush. He brings goodwill but he's not gooey, and that's a surprise. 'You Make Me Feel Like Dancing', done in falsetto, swings; 'When I Need You' (an underrated song) has the potential to be the candle-holding, sea-of-hands number of the night. But then John Paul Young comes on in drag to annoy and play up to Sayer. It's a pantomime moment, ill-judged, to be forgiven if it were a closing-night jape. But a moment is ruined and, without wishing to be cruel, it is so *Countdown*.

There are two sad omissions from the show: Skyhooks and The Ted Mulry Gang, due to the deaths of Graeme 'Shirley' Strachan and Ted Mulry. Skyhooks verses Sherbet would have been the selling point that could have tipped all of this into the realm of the supernova. Then it might have transcended the limitations of *Countdown* and truly been a Spectacular. As for Ted Mulry, his name pops up a few times during the show. Sherbet does a section of one of his songs, and guitarist Harvey James makes a small and moving speech. Mulry must have been a lovely man, and 'Jump in My Car' would have torn the place apart.

Despite the once-in-a-career opportunity to play just one or two songs and impress, some people don't. Jon English is one. Brian Canham from Pseudo Echo, taking far too much heavy guitar to 'Funkytown', is another. There are also surprises: that Sherbet has a good drummer; the dignity of John Paul Young (excepting his intrusion on Sayer's performance). And there is a disaster: Molly and Gavin. Gavin Wood's all-knowing voiceover to the bumbling Molly worked on television, and they probably thought that given the freedom of a stadium show, they could cut loose a little. Big mistake. The added space only makes them more embarrassing, and cruder. They are needed, but this is not a leagues club, and their act jars in the middle of the music.

The big draw is Sherbet, who must have resisted a number of offers over the years to reform and have now taken the plunge. They're a weird group. In another life they could have been Genesis or Queen – good-looking boys with a taste for prog rock and the ability to write hit tunes. They never seemed like a teen band, but they became one, thanks to *Countdown* as much as anything. There is a playfulness to them on stage that comes from musical competence and the fact that they are having a damn good time. Braithwaite continually glances at the set-list between songs, as if there were 30 songs they could play. The paradox is that they are the most overtly 'bubblegum' act of the night, yet they are also the loosest, the one band who could have taken it *anywhere*. They finish with 'Howzat'.

Musically, this is a good show, but it lacks context. The entire *Countdown* experience is not wrapped up and presented to the audience in a sufficiently thoughtful way. The acts come on and play, some of the more famous incidents from the series are shown on screens, and it's pretty much left at that. Someone was needed to contextualise all of this:

someone with a visual eye who could have taken the footage and the live acts and put them together in a more theatrical and meaningful manner. Too much cultural fun goes unexplored. And where was the famous Iggy Pop appearance, mentioned in the program by almost every performer as their favourite *Countdown* moment? Where were the greetings from Elton and Rod and Olivia?

Finally, there is Molly. As promoter Michael Gudinski said when he addressed the crowd after the show (where else in the world would that happen?), Molly is *Countdown*. It's true, and it makes you either want to cry or throw your head back and laugh. But that's to do with his persona, and that a man of his age was hosting a teen-oriented pop show in the first place. Behind the tomfoolery, the football fanaticism, the media tart, beats a great pop heart. It was Molly's suggestion, with the entire cast on stage, the camaraderie clearly visible after ten shows, that they finish the night with a new song written on the road. Molly knows the best way to face the past is to turn to the future.

Out on the Weekend

Vampire Weekend

The big discussion has been about Ezra's hair. Recent photos have had it fluffy and a little out of control. No problems tonight, though; it's clipped and up over the ears, with a fringe that curls just above the left eye. He's in old-school trainers sans socks, tight black trousers that don't scream 'rock', and his signature blonde Epiphone semi-acoustic guitar nestles into his shoulder. It doesn't take too long into the set, with Ezra hunched intently over the microphone, one leg pumping, to realise that this guy, much as he would squirm at the label, is a rock star. And with an all-ages crowd heavy with teenage girls – a bra at one moment flies past his face – something of a heartthrob too.

Tonight's show is one of eight in Australia, part of a world tour that will have the band in Wales in two weeks, Philadelphia in three, and then straight back to Europe to play every major rock festival of the summer. Further in the distance is three nights at Radio City Hall in hometown New York, and the Hollywood Bowl on 26 September. So Brisbane, in the old vaudevillian charm of the Tivoli Theatre, is an intimate gig, one more stop on the long trail to promote a second album that, besides reaching number one on the US charts, also follows quickly on the heels of one of the best debut albums of the last 20 years. And though the group are contained and tight, with that particular brand of New York perma-cool well in place, you'd have to say they blaze and deliver.

The quick explanation for their popularity is the catchiness and clout of the songs. They have around 20 of them and they're played well. The charm of Vampire Weekend is their lightness of touch; the space in the music and the discrimination shown in the choice of instruments that carry the tunes. Ezra Koenig sings many a verse with his hands at his side, the rhythm section of Chris Thomson (drums) and Chris Baio (bass) shake the bones of the songs but never settle into stretches of dull rock timekeeping, and Rostam Batmanglij, being the band's musical genius, is capable of weaving layers of guitar and keyboards through a song without it ever sounding intrusive. Heavy volume and the strum that fills so much rock and pop music are mostly absent, and when the foot is suddenly put to the floor to punctuate a chorus or race through an instrumental section, the effect is electrifying. Part of this ability comes from the roots of the band's music. Afro-pop, hip-hop, ska and R & B all have space and air. Vampire Weekend have added some straight pop and an indie touch in the lyrics to make a very refreshing and infectious brand of music. It's been influential too; tonight's support band, Cloud Control, is one of many groups under the spell, with the jazzy riffs and three-chord 'African' chorus of their latest single, 'This Is What I Said', as evidence.

The first half of tonight's set leans on the new album, *Contra*, with several of the up-tempo songs, 'Holiday', 'Run' and 'Giving Up the Gun', sounding stronger in the live setting. This supports a minor criticism of the record's production by band member Batmanglij, who has a tendency through talent and exuberance to overload songs with ideas; things can get a little *too* clever and cut up. The stripped-down stride the band falls into with these songs brightens and lifts them from the memory of the album versions. Other tracks, such as recent single 'Cousins' – a distant relative in punch and melody of Elvis Costello's 'Pump It Up' – and 'Horchata', impress as they do on record. And thankfully a place is found for 'Taxi Cab'. This is a trippy ballad unlike anything on their debut; coming after four up-tempo tracks, it is the kind of groundbreaking moment bands dream of for their second album.

On stage Thomson leaves his kit to play a triggered drum pad and Baio puts his Rickenbacker down to play upright bass. The song ripples over a beautiful melody and, although Vampire Weekend lyrics are always difficult to decode, Ezra seems to be inching closer to a narrative, the music bringing him there as he croons: "Unsentimental / Travelling around / Sure of myself / Sure of it now / But you were standing there so close to me / Like the future was supposed to be / In the aisles of the grocery / And the blocks uptown."

The first album's songs get their run and ignite a storm. The balcony shakes, the mosh pit swirls faster, and the boys in the band barely blink. And the strength of 'A-Punk', 'Mansard Roof', 'I Stand Corrected' and 'Oxford Comma' (best song of the last five years) can't be denied. These numbers *are* special and still very fresh-sounding, and they reinforce the relation the defiantly titled *Contra* has to its predecessor. It is an album that lacks the killer run of formation-era songs, but it is also an album from a group smart enough not to try to fake a run of such songs, nor to lean too heavily on the sonic blueprint of their debut. There is a touch of New York in this, a town that likes its artists to be successful but also to return diligently to the experimental coalface when it comes to future work. So one of the chief pleasures of the concert is to hear the smoother-than-expected join between the albums, and to find in the bones of *Contra* a set of songs closer in quality and substance to the more celebrated debut.

The band play for a crisp hour, with minimal between-song chat. Ezra manages to pronounce Brisbane as 'Brizbin' and save himself a groaning admonishment from the crowd. There is one three-song encore, which is gracefully signalled as the last music of the night. They finish on a ferocious 'Walcott', the last chorus repeated with building intensity in a rare gesture to the orthodoxies of rock. It is climax reached and then quickly left as the band walks purposefully off stage. We file out with the wind still in our chests. Best band in the world at the moment. Check. Next album to be blinding. Check.

Bowled Again ...

The Big Day Out

Brisbane is in the middle of its wettest summer in more than ten years. The rain started well before Christmas and there have barely been three days of straight sunshine since. Other cities further south swelter in the high 30s while in Brisbane it's hardly touched 30, and here we are well into 2008 with no break from the rain in sight. I am thinking of reasons why I want to go to the Big Day Out this year, and knowing that I'm not going to be baked in a caged field behind the Gold Coast is one. This year's band line-up is another, with Arcade Fire, LCD Soundsystem, Björk, Augie March and Spoon catching the eye. And then there's the feeling that I simply should – that leaving my family and suburban life for a day to take in a live-music experience with 53,000 people younger than myself just may be a good thing to do. I need to get out more.

This is my third brush with the Big Day Out, Australia's longest running (it began in 1992) and most successful rock festival. In 1994 I played the Gold Coast leg with my Brisbane band of the time. In 2001 The Go-Betweens did all the capital-city dates of the tour. Highlights were the Adelaide and Melbourne shows, and a cricket game in Perth between us, Powderfinger and Coldplay. It was held in a park beside the hotel. Fellow Go-Between Grant McLennan and I batted together for a few overs in this distinctly competitive but very friendly tippety-run match. I was bowled by a very good inswinger from the drummer from Coldplay. While we were batting came the frequent call from behind the stumps, "Come on! We've got to get these Go-Betweens out!" The wicket-keeper was Bernard Fanning. These are treasured memories.

I enter to Enter Shikari. They are from England, they are on the

Converse Essential Stage and they are playing a ska-driven form of dark metal. Half the crowd is giving them the splayed-finger devil sign while the other half laughs. They are awful and it's 2.30 in the afternoon. Next up is Spoon. They are on the Green Stage, where in an hour and a half I will see Augie March. Spoon come from Texas with a big reputation. I have heard the odd track of theirs but no albums. Perhaps the 40-minute festival set-list doesn't suit them, or not today at least. They zigzag from a splintered kind of dubby rock to a Euro-disco track to some Big Star guitar pop, and it doesn't all fit. They have some good songs and some good bits of songs, but the singer–songwriter seemed like he couldn't be arsed and the awkward jamming of styles never builds to a coherent strategy for trying to win an audience over. I leave after 30 minutes.

Lack of enthusiasm is not a problem for Yves Klein Blue. They are a bunch of 19 and 20-year-olds from Brisbane who are grabbing the chance of playing the Big Day Out by the neck. It's pop with fierce rhythms – and they have songs. Being of tender age they tend to swerve madly between styles, and not all of it comes off. Energy and a cool belief get them through, though. There is a ring of young ladies in the front row staring at the handsome lead singer; the drummer is in a poncho. Up here on the hill at the Local Produce stage, watching them with the 300 indie kids that have braved the day, a positive of the festival emerges. The different tents and areas cut off the different musical and stylistic subcultures, giving you a taste of a world within walking distance of another world. How different these cultures are becomes apparent the moment I step into the Boiler Room. Jesus! It's a dance party. Here are 10,000 beautiful people with very little clothing on. On stage are Pnau and the moment someone walks on to join them dressed as a strawberry (I'm not making this up), the whole place goes fucking nuts. It's a throbbing, ecstatic mass of people listening to throbbing, ecstatic music. I stand there amid the crowd and experience the one moment of pure exhilaration I will feel all day. The sound is a rush that works on climbing levels to a juddering plateau which I can only describe as the musical equivalent of permanent orgasm; and then it suddenly drops, to start the build all over again.

I want Augie March to be brilliant. They start with a ballad, then peel off three magnificent songs from their last album, *Moo, You Bloody Choir*, and something's wrong. The bass is taking up at least half the sound, in its wake crushing singer–songwriter Glenn Richards' voice back in the mix. Dynamics are lost and great songs don't shine as they should, forcing Richards to complain of the loud whooshing bass sound he is hearing on stage. It is a tragedy – and bewildering given that Spoon, who played before them, had a crystal-clear mix coming through the speakers. The case could be made for Oz-rock heavy-handedness on the sound desk, as the bass drum is too loud and the whole kit sounds rough and clunky. What gets lost is the voice of potentially the best rock singer in Australia, who has with him a swooning batch of songs that need light and space. Watching them, you yearn for an acoustic guitar in someone's hands, an upright bass maybe, and a touch more old-style rock piano. But all of this could be the sound problems of one day, and the full-electric approach they have might work perfectly somewhere else.

The minute Arcade Fire walk on stage, it starts to rain. Their fans would see this as some form of mystical collusion between the gods and the music their favourite band plays. I am caught too far back when they start and spend the rest of the time they are on stage trying to rectify this disadvantage. The sound this Canadian ten-piece is making is simply not hitting me in the chest and watching from a distance of 80 metres, with the band members throwing themselves at their instruments, makes their performance look like bad pantomime. I have to get closer. I use my backstage pass and suddenly I am on stage with them. Actually, I'm at the side of the stage and while I can now see them very clearly, the sound is bad. So I venture out again and watch from a fenced area to the side, and still there is not enough connection to the band. Finally, I jump a fence and join a section of non-drinking audience members in front of the stage and then the band is framed, the sound is right, but unfortunately they are on their second-last number. What are they like? It's tough to tell. I know and enjoy their two albums, *Funeral* and *Neon Bible*, and they perform all the best songs from them. It comes down to how you take the almost exaggerated zeal with which they play. I'm left feeling less impressed than I thought I'd be, and yet remain a believer.

Daniel Johns from Silverchair has jammed his guitar up against his amp stack and it's feeding back. He turns to his foot switches and the sound squeals. It's a big rock 'n' roll ending to their set and in its way a perfect introduction to Björk, who arrives on the adjacent stage with the intention of subverting, or just gleefully dancing around, some rock 'n' roll clichés. She is great tonight. I've had Björk in the too-silly category for a while. The large brass section marching on at the start of the performance is expected; the boffins on keyboards and laptop computers are expected; the costumes and face paint she and the brass players have on is expected too. The surprise (and it shouldn't be) is the serious artist in the middle of all this. Björk is the one performer I see today who kicks away the props, the noise and the standard theatrics, to hold a stage with her talent and musical brain. The songs are slowish, with a very cunning mix of electronic beats and melody rubbing up against the old-school feel of the brass section. Reigning atop the band is her voice, stacks of reverb on it, and her delivery is sensitive and precise. She is impressive. She dances and twirls and sings lyrics like "I will go hunting" or "How very Scandinavian of me", and it's not tricky or gimmicky but real on a day with much posturing and blasting.

The man who is organising the transport to and from the Big Day Out uses the word 'fuck' at least once in every sentence. He tells me, "This place is a fuckin' nightmare if you leave too late. It will take you two fuckin' hours just to get out of here," as he points down the road. He's a jovial person and I believe him. So I decide to leave now, instead of staying to the bitter end. It means I miss headliners Rage Against the Machine, who I didn't want to see anyway, and LCD Soundsystem, who I did. They are playing in the Boiler Room and, remembering what it was like at four in the afternoon, I can only wonder what scenes are going down there five hours later. Also, the tent is in something of a gully, and with the amount of people there it would be very difficult to see the stage. It's the one regret of the day, but – with 53,000 people under very dark clouds – I get on the bus and go.

Strangers in the Night

Roberta Flack & Leonard Cohen

First there was *First Take*, one of the best debut albums of all time. It was recorded by Roberta Flack in 1969 for Atlantic Records, produced by Joel Dorn, with a backing trio that included jazz giant Ron Carter on bass. Flack was 32 when she cut it, coming late to a recording career after years as a music and English teacher, a piano accompanist to other singers, and finally stints on her own in nightclubs – the most famous being Mr Henry's in Washington, DC, where in the mid-to-late '60s she knocked together a career-shaping set of songs that ranged across pop, jazz, gospel and folk. *First Take* is where an eclectic repertoire, a cool and soaring voice, and a funky, minimal group met under the direction of a producer who knew when to bring in the strings and the brass, and when to leave Flack alone to impress with her singing, piano playing and song selection.

The songs were the key, for Flack has not been able to find or gather a similarly audacious and satisfying collection of material since. Whether she picked the eyes out of the rumoured 42 songs she auditioned with, or conservatism subsequently crept into her song choices, *First Take* is an album she has never bettered, a place where lightning struck once. It included the hit 'The First Time Ever I Saw Your Face', but on an album this strong it can only earn a place deep in side two. The opening side is the showcase, a four-song knockout starting with Gene McDaniels' funky and uncompromising 'Compared to What' ("Nobody gives us rhyme or reason / Have one doubt, they call it treason") before dropping into the gorgeous, aching roll of 'Angelitos Negroes', which Flack sings in Spanish; this is followed by the start of a long relationship with the music of Donny Hathaway on his 'Our Ages or Our Hearts', and finally by the mind-blowing intensity of 'I Told Jesus', the song and side ending appropriately enough with a pause and a crash. This is draining music, and it can make turning the record over a brave decision. If you do, the first song you'll hear is Leonard Cohen's 'Hey, That's No Way to Say Goodbye'; it's the only pop song on the album and the only number that comes in under five minutes. This is a record where Leonard Cohen is the light relief.

Cohen was in Brisbane the night before Flack in early February this year, performing at the same venue, and he sang 'Hey, That's No Way to Say Goodbye' with the affection and attention to detail that he brought to everything he did that evening. I wondered if he'd mention Flack's version or her performing the next night, but he didn't, and she didn't perform the song. Cohen and Flack were big ships passing close over the two nights, and the difference between their performances and their relationship to their best-known work, much of which was forged in the fire of the late '60s and early '70s, is intriguing.

Flack got her commercial breakthrough when jazz-buff Clint Eastwood, while listening to a West-Coast station, heard the album version of 'The First Time Ever I Saw Your Face' and put it on the soundtrack to his directorial debut, *Play Misty for Me*. It helped break the song. 'Killing Me Softly with His Song' and 'Feel Like Making Love' followed; 'Where Is the Love?' was a smash sung with Donny Hathaway. By now, Flack's albums were slicker and selling, but in the late '70s earthy balladry was on the way out and her career cooled. As for Leonard Cohen, it has been a strange ride: albums appearing at irregular intervals, underground-hero status remaining intact, unexpected bankruptcy throwing him back on the road for the first time in almost 16 years, while 'Hallelujah', written in the early '80s, is a worldwide hit in the hands of young pretenders. For Cohen, now 74, the future is looking very bright.

Roberta Flack walks on wearing black and a gold sparkling jacket, and – with Derek Hughes, one of her two male back-up singers – opens with 'Where Is the Love?'. It is a welcoming move and there is further reassurance when she sits down at the piano and does a funky version of 'Sweet Georgia Brown'. Her voice is classy and warm, and her bubbly chat is engaging. But alarm bells start ringing one song later when, during Goffin and King's 'Will You Still Love Me Tomorrow?' (a song covered beautifully on Flack's third album, *Quiet Fire*), she stops singing at the end of the verse and asks the audience to perform the chorus. Whispered voices flutter around, people having paid up to $150 for a ticket now finding themselves carrying the fourth number of the night. Next, we get a song from the movie *Tootsie* – "you know, the one with Dustin Hoffman in drag" – and then she's off. "It really is an interval," a surprised woman beside me says to her partner as the lights come up. Out in the foyer the mood is subdued: no one is going to riot, but there is little buzz.

She is back, bang on the hour, presumably knowing that the second half of the show has to be more substantial than the first. 'Tonight, I Celebrate My Love', a big romantic ballad, is good and her voice, though noticeably shaky on some of the high notes, is gorgeous in the middle range. 'Feel Like Makin' Love' is also sung well, but by now it is obvious the songs aren't building to anything; the scattered approach to her back catalogue and the showbizzy between-song patter is not carrying the audience along. Warm applause breaks out at the first notes of 'Killing Me Softly with His Song': this and 'The First Time Ever' are what the audience has primarily come to hear. The best way for an artist to treat their greatest hits, it seems, is to play it straight and be enthusiastic. On 'Killing Me Softly' Flack does neither; the performance is lacklustre, with the back-up vocalists carrying the chorus's high notes; a bossa-nova coda only manages to reduce the applause for this '70s classic to a low rumble. In keeping with the unpredictability of the night, Flack follows up with the show's highlight. There are 189 recorded Beatles songs, she tells us, and she has recorded what feels like half of them for a still-to-be-completed album for Sony. She then plays 'Here Comes the Sun' and it's great. For the first time tonight she is hunched over the piano and concentrating, just as she is on the cover of *First Take*.

Thirty-five minutes into the second set and suddenly we are into an encore, with the band vamping and the two back-up singers swinging their arms to get the crowd to cheer louder for Flack to come back on stage. It is embarrassing. She sits down at the piano for – what else? – 'The First Time Ever', done better and with more heart than 'Killing Me Softly', though we get the shorter version of the song. Before the final number and second encore (more desperate hand-waving from the singers), she tells us she has sinus problems, and it's a hint of an apology. She ends with the Pretenders' 'I'll Stand By You', which has more audience participation, and then she's gone. With the comings and goings, band introductions, between-song chat and paucity of singing, it doesn't require much calculation to see that while Flack has got by, she has not been at all generous.

The contrast with Leonard Cohen's show was stark. Cohen cared, and it showed in every decision he made, starting with his band. They looked hand-picked and happy to be there. Flack tacked on the Queensland Orchestra (and other state orchestras as she travelled Australia) to her six-piece group, and while not being awkward there was no noticeable empathy between band and orchestra, either musically or in spirit. Cohen was all spirit; part of the shine may have come from not having toured for so many years, but he let his talent infuse the show, and the crowd knew it. He carried 9000 people and made a vast stadium feel like a bohemian club. He did it by isolating the essence of what he does, presenting it with graciousness and seriousness and delicious cap-in-hand self-deprecation. Flack leant on show business, which can be an unsteady rail, especially when you're giving off the vibe that you're rushing and don't really want to be there. It catches up with you, so you end up in the middle of songs yelling out, "Come on, Brisbane!" – something Leonard Cohen didn't have to do. He just smiled and bowed, aware that he had a closet full of great songs and was going to do justice to them all over three hours. There was fire in his eyes when he sang 'Suzanne', pain and commitment when called for in other songs, and there were no short cuts; just an artist treating his back catalogue not as hits and misses but as signposts and reportage on the stations of life. That he can triumphantly return at 74 and do this may be the reason for the spring in his step as he leapt on and off the stage.

Roberta Flack could do this, too. Twenty songs, her at the piano, bass and drums, a horn player maybe, no tricks but a program she believed in, and we'd follow her up the mountain as well. With any luck she'll finish that Beatles album and it will be a big success. The clever arrangement of 'Here Comes the Sun' shows she hasn't lost the ability to take a song ingrained in popular consciousness and spin it into a new dimension. Then, she might come back to live performance enthused and focused, which would be a joy, because the show she did this time was no way to say goodbye.

ON GRANT

A True Hipster

On 6 May, on a Saturday afternoon while preparing a house-warming party, Grant McLennan, a friend and working partner of mine for 30 years, died of a heart attack. He was 48 years old. This is a remembrance.

Grant and I started the Brisbane band The Go-Betweens in January 1978. We'd met two years earlier in the drama department at the University of Queensland, where we were both doing Bachelor of Arts degrees centred mainly on English literature. Most of the drama subjects were taught at a small off-campus theatre called the Avalon. It was a jostling atmosphere in which Grant and I felt immediately at home, and our friendship began and blossomed here, amid the costume trunks, the works of Beckett, Genet and Ionesco (perfect for a pop band), and a genial professor, an Englishman by the name of Harry Garlick. It was action, and fun, and good learning, and it's where The Go-Betweens started.

Grant was a whiz-kid when I first met him. His passion was film. He was going to be either a director or the greatest film critic this country had ever seen. At 18, he was writing reviews for a publication called *Cinema Papers*, while working at the Schonell, the campus cinema where he assisted with the programming. At 19, he'd done his BA. It was as if he'd raced so hard, and with such brilliance, that he'd got slightly ahead of himself. His application for the film and television school in Sydney was turned down on the grounds that he was too young. Which is where I came in, to fill a gap that was to be merely a year or two, before further adventures took us elsewhere.

While Grant had been pouring himself into film, I'd been falling into music. My academic record at university was patchy beside his. I never finished the degree. The electric guitar and stirrings overseas sighted in the music press were starting to consume me. Grant knew I had a band with a university friend and a drummer, and this intrigued him. The band, which went under two names, The Mosquitoes (taken from *Gilligan's Island*) and The Godots (from Beckett), only did three shows over two years, of which Grant saw the last two. At the final show, we played the first good song I thought I'd written. It was called 'Karen'.

The similarities between us were strong. We were both private-school boys who'd done well academically but come out of the system with no idea of a career. We were both looking for something that bohemian-free Brisbane couldn't offer, except in the traditional safety of an Arts degree. And we were both uneasy and difficult, having emerged from families who looked on somewhat bewildered at the eldest sons they had produced. When Grant and I met, we didn't know it but we'd found each other. Rough mirror-images. And when the friendship that had begun in classes grew to the point where I visited his house and saw his bedroom stacked with film books, novels and posters, I realised his 'thing' – film – wasn't just an enthusiasm; it was an obsession. And I knew that was exactly how I felt about music.

We began a slow exchange. He told me about French new wave cinema and film noir. I told him about the greatness of The Velvet Underground. He told me about auteur theory and the genius of Preston Sturges. I told him about Dylan in the mid '60s. He mentioned Godard and Truffaut. We became Godard and Truffaut. Brisbane didn't know it at the time, but there were two 19-year-olds driving around in a car who thought they were French film directors.

So we started the band when he accepted my offer to teach him bass guitar. But it was more than that. It was the decision to pool our ambitions and resources and go for something greater than ourselves, and in this we were aided by one piece of luck: Grant was musical. He could have remained a film student who played the bass, but instead he quickly became a musician. He had a fantastic singing voice and a perfect melodic knack, unknown when I asked him to start the group. What I did know was that, given his obvious creative tendencies, he would write songs. That it took only six weeks surprised me. But after such a short time, he showed me a bass riff, I wrote a chorus, and it became the first Forster/McLennan composition. It was called 'Big Sleeping City' and we played it for a year.

Being in a band and releasing our first single – 'Lee Remick' / 'Karen' in September 1978 – gave us a certain instant notoriety, which we both enjoyed. For Grant it gave him things at 20 that a film career mightn't have handed him until he was 30: recognition, creative adventure, the instant smell that we were going places. The journey had begun. The first vial of our friendship was put aside and we became The Go-Betweens. And from then on we set off on the crusade, with the band as first priority in our lives. We travelled, recorded, added and lost members, and built up the best body of work we could until we crashed 11 years later. Occasionally, through these years, Grant and I would catch each other's eye – as we flew into New York, or played a big Danish rock festival, or went on a French TV show – and think, this is what we did it for, these pop-moment milestones that both of us had dreamed of back in Brisbane, at the beginning.

Through all of this we stayed good friends. There was something special about our friendship that we could take deep into our work, making crucial creative decisions along the way and never flaring up or tearing at each other. We operated on two rules: each was to have the same number of songs on every album, and we both had to agree on something before we did it. Our confidence in what we could do was amazing. It was as if being in The Go-Betweens gave us an invisible shield, allowing us to believe that nothing could knock us out. Grant was central to this. Every album was "our best so far", and any time I dipped in confidence he was there to pick me up. He was a great working partner. Not only the songs – 'Cattle and Cane', 'Bachelor Kisses', 'Bye Bye Pride', 'Streets of Your Town', 'Finding You', 'Boundary Rider' – but also as an up-close inspirational artist in my life.

This is what he was like. I'd drive over to his place to play guitar and he'd be lying on a bed reading a book. Grant never felt guilt about this. The world turned and worked; he read. That was the first message. He'd offer to make coffee, and I knew – and here's one of the great luxuries of my life – I knew I could ask him anything, on any artistic frontier, and he'd have an answer. He had an encyclopaedic mind of the arts, with his own personal twist. So, as he worked on the coffee, I could toss in anything I liked – something that had popped up in my life that I needed his angle on. I'd say, "Tell me about Goya," or "What do you know about Elizabeth Bishop's poetry?" or "Is the Youth Group CD any good?" And, his head over the kitchen table, he'd arch an eyebrow just to ascertain that I was serious, which I always was. Then he'd start. Erudite, logical, authoritative and never condescending – not one ounce of superiority came with the dispensing of his opinion. God. I'm going to miss that. And of all the holes his departing has left, this for me is the biggest: the person you can go to who is so much on your wavelength, stocked with shared experience, whom you don't ask for life advice –

Grant would be one of the last people there! – but who, as a fellow artist, you can go toe to toe with and always come away totally inspired by. Well, that's a great thing.

And it wasn't only me. Since his death, his role as inspirer and informer has come out strongly in remembrance. An old friend, Steve Haddon, says, "Meeting Grant in 1976 was like getting an education." Another friend, Andrew Wilson, writes, "Thank you for playing 'Johnny Jewel', *Blonde on Blonde* and Jane Birkin to me in a wooden Spring Hill room." Of the 1500 responses that quickly sprung up on the internet, many spoke of a meeting with Grant, in a bar, a café, somewhere in the world, when he told them something of someone – made an inspired artistic connection, a tip that these people carried with them. His place here is as a true hipster, in the 1940s and '50s sense of the word. Someone perched on the streets, in the saloons, on the lower side of life, possessing razor-sharp and deep knowledge of the cultural front – but never lording it in the traditional manner. Half jokingly, I once suggested he return to academia. He laughed the idea off, preferring to be the secret holder of wisdom "on a barstool throne".

The break-up of the band in 1989 was savage and abrupt. Grant and I had had enough. We'd written six lauded albums and the band was broke. In the end, we were doing Sydney pub gigs to pay ourselves wages. It was a nasty treadmill. Grant and I had planned to go on as a duo and do an acoustic album, but this got blown sky-high when his girlfriend left him on the day he told her that the band was over. The next weeks were chaos. Grant was destroyed. I stayed, consoling him and trying to make sense of the mess that we had brought on by trying to gain our freedom. But then I had to follow my own heart and return to Germany, where I'd found the beginnings of a new life over the last six months. The duo idea hit the rocks when Grant informed the record company he wanted a solo career. The fact that he told them before me hurt. But he had a girlfriend to try and win back, and this coloured many of his decisions over the next years.

For the remainder of the decade we had fulfilling solo careers. It was great to work alone and grow. There were letters and calls between us, uneasy given the differences between our new worlds – him in the cauldron, me in the Bavarian countryside. We both felt happy to have the band behind us, immensely proud of the work we'd done, but drained from all that it had taken out of us. When my first solo album, *Danger in the Past*, came out I didn't even want to leave the house. There was only one show in Australia: in Sydney, where Grant joined me. Professionally, that's what we did together for the remainder of the decade; every 18 months or so, an offer would come in from some part of the world, attractive enough for Grant and me to do a one-off acoustic show together, catch up, and then go back to our own lives.

There was one other thing, though: the film script. This was a crazy dream dating back to the late '70s. When Grant and I started working together, The Go-Betweens was to be the calling card, the most visible and instantly attractive thing we did. Behind it, we had a number of other ideas we were going to unleash upon the world once the band was famous, which our 20-year-old minds figured would be in about three years. It was the Orson Welles theory: get famous at one thing, and then bring on everything else you can do. So there was a film and a book in the wings. The film was a jewel-heist caper set on the Gold Coast and then Sydney, a vehicle aimed at our favourite American actor of the time, James Garner. The book was going to be a microscopic dissection and ode to our favourite pop star of all time, Bob Dylan, and it was going to be called *The Death of Modern America: Bob Dylan 1964–66* (which still rings like a great line to me).

Neither got beyond rough fragments, though the wish to write a film together stayed. So, in 1995, with both of us back in Brisbane, we spent three months in the bowels of the Dendy cinema in George Street writing a film called *Sydney Creeps*. It was wonderful being in a room together working on something other than music, though the script is not as good as it should be. The wrestling over each line and plot twist robbed it of flow and a strong voice. Still, it was done, and there it was: a thick notebook written in longhand, many lines crossed out and written over, lying in a trunk of Grant's last possessions.

We reconvened the band in 2000. Over the next six years we recorded three albums, toured, and took the whole thing, to our great pleasure, up another level. We were on the cusp of something. It's strange to say that about a band that had existed for 17 years, but with Adele and Glenn – our bass player and drummer – by our side, all doors still felt open. We were still up for the championship, and we had a growing audience willing us on to bigger and better things. And we had new songs: Grant had a fantastic batch for an album we were going to do next year. I said to him that all my writing up until the recording would just be catching up to what he had. Album number ten was going to be something special.

Yet he wasn't happy. He was proud of the band's recent success, and his private life, after a long bumpy ride, was settled. He was in love, and the most content and up I'd seen him in a long time. But deep down there remained a trouble, a missing piece that he was always trying to find but never did. Family, a loving girlfriend, a circle of friends: all could count for so much, and it *was* a hell of a lot, but it could never cover over a particular hurt. When Grant was four, his father died. Perhaps it stemmed from this. The missing father, the anchor that would have kept him in friendlier waters and, maybe, on narrower paths through his life. He cut a lonely figure. He was sad. Sometimes I would visit him and it would take me an hour to pull him out. Twice in his life I was with him when he was totally shattered. And there were many years I missed when we weren't in the same city.

I can remember being hit by the lyrics he put to his first songs. I was shocked by their melancholy and the struggle for joy. I'd known the happy-go-lucky university student. As soon as he wrote, there it was. Any appreciation or remembrance of Grant has to take this into account. He didn't parade it, but it's all over his work, and it was in his eye.

His refuge was art and a romantic nature that made him very lovable, even if he did take it to ridiculous degrees. Here was a man who, in 2006, didn't drive; who owned no wallet or watch, no credit card, no computer. He would only have to hand in his mobile phone and bankcard to be able to step back into the gas-lit Paris of 1875, his natural home. I admired this side of him a great deal, and it came to be part of the dynamic of our pairing. He called me 'the strategist'. He was the dreamer. We both realised, and came to relish, the perversity of the fact that this was an exact reversal of the perception people had of us as artists and personalities in the band – that I was the flamboyant man out of time and Grant the sensible rock. In reality, the opposite was true.

The last time I saw him was about two weeks before he died. The circumstances of the visit were the same as they'd been for almost 30 years: to play guitar together and do the catch-up with an old friend. He had a two-storey granny flat at the back of the house he lived in, and we played on a small deck there. A railroad track runs behind the house, and occasionally trains passed through the songs. We took breaks from the playing, and talked; we had such fun together. Talking. Always talking and gossiping – silly stuff we'd go round and round on.

After four hours I left. He was standing on the front veranda as I walked down to the front gate. In the mailbox was a wrapped copy of the *New York Review of Books*. I took it out and looked at the cover. I called to him, saying I didn't know he got this. He told me he had a subscription, and if I wanted to I could borrow back-issues. I thanked him, said I would and then said goodbye. As I walked to the car and got in, I wondered how many singer–songwriters or rock stars in the world got the *New York Review of Books* delivered on subscription. Not many, I thought. Maybe just one.

We had started on our tenth album. It had begun the same way as all the others. I went over to his place during the day and we'd play the songs each of us had written.

I'd find him in either of two locations: pottering around the kitchen or lying on his bed, reading. The first ten minutes would always be a little tetchy. Although we'd known each other for almost 30 years and worked closely together for a good half of that time, he'd be a little gruff; it was as if, each time I saw him, he had to get to know me again. So, he'd make coffee and I'd sit in a chair in the kitchen and pepper him with questions in an attempt to bring him around to good humour. This is where having known him for such a long time helped, because I knew the buttons to push, the silly things to say, the cheeky remark about an album he liked, the films of a certain actor I'd know he'd trash, a bit of local rock-scene gossip. Anything really, and after ten minutes, he'd be the person I'd always known.

Then we'd play guitar together – his new songs and mine, which built a world we'd then shape, record and send out to those who loved or liked what we did. It was the tenth album we were shooting for. We were just two months into it, eight songs written, when he died.

The group is The Go-Betweens and 'he' is Grant McLennan. We'd started the band in 1978 when we met as Art students at Queensland University. He was the film nut who passed every exam and who, at 18, was programming the campus cinema. I was flailing my way through courses with a 50% failure rate, my mind too taken up by the *NME*, import records and the fumbled desire to express myself through songwriting. We became best friends and, two years later, I convinced

Grant to learn bass, to learn my songs, and to fall into the dream of being just 20 and in a rock band.

Quickly, Grant started to write songs, too. I knew he would – given he was the most switched-on and creative person I'd come across. So there were two singer–songwriters in the band and, over the next 11 years, we took the group as far as we could. People joined and left. Six albums were made. For five years, we lived in London and did as well as any Australian band could hope to do without hitting the big time of platinum-selling albums and arena-filling tours.

Maybe that made us lucky. It meant Grant and I could walk away from the band in 1989 and still be friends, still be sane and still have the determination to make good solo albums. It also meant we weren't stamped with the 1980s. No reunion tours with Culture Club beckoned.

This all helped when we restarted the group in 2000. With musician friends Adele Pickvance on bass and Glenn Thompson on drums, we made three more albums, the last being 2005's *Oceans Apart*. By then, the whole thing was on an upswing. We got five-star reviews and our first music award. With another album approaching, Grant and I could feel the momentum and goodwill. We were writing well: it felt as if, with our most recent three albums, we were on a run, as we had been in the 1980s. And then it all changed in a day.

Grant died of a heart attack on 6 May 2006. He was 48. Others lost a brother, son, lover, cousin, acquaintance. I lost my best male friend and my working partner: the one who'd been with me through countless performances, studios, rehearsals, airports, tour buses, bad television shows, hard-to-find radio stations, songwriting bedrooms and kitchens; the one I thought I still had a future with. Our band finished the day he died. I knew that instantly. What remained were shock waves of grief and days on my veranda trying to make sense of it all and of what I was going to do next.

We had the eight songs. Two of them I had written; the other six were Grant's. One of his was 'Demon Days'. I remember him phoning me up in late January to say I should come over and hear some new songs. There was excitement in his voice. I went over late one night, which was unusual because we always played during the day. He lived in a small two-storey tower at the back of a house, and I climbed the stairs to his bedroom, where he'd set out two chairs. He then played me three songs. Two of them were amazing, and one in particular, 'Demon Days', I immediately thought was one of the best four or five he'd ever written. It was a waltz ballad, and as he strummed and sang it, with a beautiful instrumental section included, I looked at him in wonder. And I'm glad that at that moment, as the room went still, I said: "For the next 18 months, I'm going to be writing just to catch up with you." He laughed, but it was true.

The reason *The Evangelist* exists is partly due to my determination to record 'Demon Days' and bring it to the world. There were other great songs he had, two of which I took for the album. Our collaboration went on after his passing in that he had not finished the lyrics to any of those three songs. 'Demon Days' was the most complete, with a chorus and five lines written of the first verse; the other two songs, 'Let Your Light In, Babe' and 'It Ain't Easy', had chorus lyrics only. For 'Let Your Light In, Babe', I constructed a narrative that had come to me after reading a nineteenth-century poem of erotic romance set in a church. 'It Ain't Easy' was harder to write. I settled on a portrait of him, something detailed that played off against the quick pop feel of the melody. I wrote eight verses before I hit one that started "And a river ran, and a train ran, and a dream ran through everything that he did". I liked this. So I started the song with it.

There were my songs also. Some Grant knew, as I had played them with him; others he would never know.

The writing of the first song after Grant's passing was a moment that had to come. A breakthrough came in August, when I wrote the title song, 'The Evangelist'. The song crept up on me and just unfolded in one day. I wrote it with relief, and with joy, because I could see it was a big song, the kind you hope to have two or three of on any given record.

I wrote another song, and then it was time to phone Adele, the bass player, who lived ten minutes away from me in Brisbane, and to start playing the songs with her. By now, it was the new year. We would sit side by side. I'd say, "Here's 'Demon Days'," and play it to her. Then, "Here's 'The Evangelist'." Then, "Here's 'Let Your Light In, Babe'." And a new process started up. Adele, whom I'd known and played with for 13 years, became the other person with me now: kicking off ideas for arrangements, listening to the songs and commenting, and singing along on the choruses.

Where to record the album, and with whom, was the biggest question. One impulse was to run: find a shed somewhere by the beach or out in the bush, drag an eight-track in there, make a howl and a seeming fresh start somewhere far away. But I went with Adele and Glenn back to London. Back to Lower Norwood, in fact, where the producers Mark Wallis and Dave Ruffy have a studio and where we recorded the previous Go-Betweens record in 2005.

That decision worked. We recorded together knowing a piece was missing, but that we were all happy working together on the thing that happened after the piece went missing. Grant's ghost was there, but there weren't too many sad moments. Process, and the day-to-day work that goes into making an album, robbed us of too much reflection. His amp was set up and a guitar of his stood on a stand. We all had to work a bit faster because Grant's turn to sing or play never came around. Through it all, though, we knew we were honouring him by making a great record in a place that he knew.

We did 'Demon Days', and I think we did it justice. On the night Grant had first played it to me, we had talked of strings and one name had come up: Audrey Riley. Audrey had done the string arrangements on our fourth album, *Liberty Belle and the Black Diamond Express*, which we'd recorded in London back in 1985. They were the first string arrangements she'd done. After us, her career bloomed (this often happened to people who worked with us) and you'll now see her name gracing Coldplay and Foo Fighters records.

Audrey and the other members of her quartet came to the studio on the allotted day. Three of the quartet (including Audrey) had played on *Liberty Belle* 22 years ago. Circles were being completed. Grant had been close and then far away through the recording. As we heard the gorgeous flowing lines that Audrey had written, at that moment, bows on strings, strings on wood, he was right there in the room.

OTHER WRITINGS

Guy Clark's *Old No. 1*

There's an argument to be made that no one should be allowed into a recording studio until they are 30 years of age. Novelists, playwrights, artists and filmmakers usually have to wait that long before having their first major publication or significant showing of their work, so why not recording artists? It would allow for the maturing of technique and the life experience that other artists must assimilate and then translate into 'voice', and it would give the listening audience a break from the adolescent romance, complaint and obvious revelation that still pervades most rock music – debut rock or pop albums especially. Imagine someone coming along who had lived. Someone with a failed marriage behind him, who had travelled and worked with his hands in a number of cities, and whose childhood was sufficiently distant to be romanticised or even understood. Imagine all of this sung about in a warm and knowing voice to killer tunes written by the singer on an acoustic guitar, and that the music to these songs took the honesty and craft of folk music, the best of country-music melodies, and then doused it with a wry 'rock' attitude that borders on hippy but in some bizarre way predates the bitten reality of Raymond Carver. This person is Guy Clark. He made *Old No. 1* in 1975 at the age of 34. It may not be the best debut album of all time – but it's damn close.

Guy Clark was born in the small West Texas town of Monahans in 1941. It's oil-well country, remote and bare, resembling – you would imagine – the dusty motion-picture landscape of *Giant* or *The Last Picture Show*. Two songs would pop up on *Old No. 1* directly inspired by this faraway time and setting: 'Texas – 1947' and 'Desperados Waiting for the Train'. By the early 1960s Clark was in Houston playing guitar in folk clubs, having ditched the more obvious middle-class career paths of medicine or law, the latter practised by his father. Clark joined the Peace Corps briefly, he built and repaired guitars, and moved in the stream of the Houston folk boom, meeting future hero singer–songwriters Jerry Jeff Walker and Townes Van Zandt and all the while continuing to sing and play Bob Dylan and traditional songs in coffee houses. 1969 found him in San Francisco catching the ugly end of the Summer of Love; and the following year he was back in Houston working as an art director for a local television channel. But by now it was decision time, and with the support of his second wife Susanna Clark and with the quality of the songs he had begun to write rising, they moved out to Los Angeles, where he wrote his first great song – the first for *Old No. 1* – 'That Old Time Feeling'. It was 1971, and while working in the Dobro guitar factory by day, Clark wrote and hustled his growing bag of songs around Tinseltown, finally scoring an RCA publishing deal that resulted in a move to Nashville.

Old No. 1 was recorded there, and in the four years between his arrival and the making of the album, Clark had some of his best songs covered by other artists. The Everly Brothers did 'Nickel for the Fiddler', and old pal Jerry Jeff Walker, famous for having written 'Mr Bojangles', would be the first to record 'Desperados Waiting for the Train', 'That Old Time Feeling' and 'LA Freeway', which he would turn into a minor hit. But Clark was not a natural fit for Nashville; he'd seen and done too much, and his songs told this story and not the tales of cheating husbands and wives that were the bread and butter of the country-music songwriter. He did attract followers, though; young songwriters such as Rodney Crowell and a very young Steve Earle, drawn to country music but repelled by its restrictions, and in awe of the weight and majesty of the songs Clark was now gathering for a debut album. *Old No. 1* was recorded twice, in circumstances that still remain obscure. A producer was hired and a version recorded and abandoned; high-quality demo versions were then used and tidied up. For an album so complete and sturdy, it had a shaky birth.

There are ten songs on the record and they are sequenced and carefully divided, as was the custom of the time, into a 'side one' and a 'side two'. The album begins with, or more literally the door to the record is kicked open by, 'Rita Ballou', and it's only fitting that she's a "rawhide rope and velvet mixture / Walkin' talkin' Texas texture / High-timin' barroom fixture / Kind of a girl" – which, with the omission of the last line, could be a description of the hard-living, shoot-from-the-hip style of Clark himself. Then comes the introductory guitar riff of 'LA Freeway' and its extraordinarily evocative opening lines:

Pack up all your dishes
Make note of all good wishes
Say goodbye to the landlord for me
That son of a bitch has always bored me

How's that for atmosphere? And the tune and the singing and the stirring swell of the instruments don't let the words down. 'LA Freeway' is really something. Written after Clark's Los Angeles sojourn, it's a kiss-off to a city and a way of life, name-checking friends – 'Skinny Dennis' – left behind, stacked with good detail, and able to dispense some sweet philosophy along the way: "Love's a gift that's surely handmade". It's a hymn to movement and belief, its story being the train of events that got Guy and Susanna out of the dread of LA and on the road to *Old No. 1* itself.

'She Ain't Goin' Nowhere' has often been cited by Guy Clark as the favourite of his songs. It's easy to see why – there's a neatness and economy to the lyric and melody that give the three-minute song a sense of perfection, which would please the craftsman in him. Coming after 'LA Freeway', and echoing that song's notions of noble independence and departure, with "Standin' on the gone side of leaving" as its opening line, it makes for a very strong two-song punch early in the album. Of course, as with all great records the sequencing is just right, so the snappy and sweet 'A Nickel for the Fiddler' follows, or, more aptly, races by. It's another great tune, with some flying lines – "It's a nickel for the tambourine kind of afternoon" – but breath is being drawn for 'That Old Time Feeling'. There was a mood in the air at the time – John Prine caught it too, on songs such as 'Donald and Lydia' from his first album – that had early-'70s songwriters finding a poignancy in older people and the rigours they had endured with the passing of time. What the 'old-time feeling' actually is, the song doesn't make clear: it's a feeling, but it's to do with "an old grey cat in winter keepin' close to the wall", "old women with no children holdin' hands with the clock" and "an old man with his checkers, dying to find a game". Great, great song, and when I saw Clark perform in Berlin in 1990 and he called out for requests, I asked for this, and he played it.

Side two starts with 'Texas – 1947', and what is remarkable is that this side may be better than its predecessor. Clark can do narrative, and 'Texas – 1947' – what a bold and brilliant title – shows his skill at cutting and shaping a tale, as well as judging the scope and size of the stories he wishes to tell. What we get in three minutes and ten seconds is a reconstruction, through the eyes of a six-year-old, of a train ("a fast-rollin' streamline") passing through an isolated country town in rural

Texas, and the excitement and commotion that such an event brings to a community. Next up is 'Desperados Waiting for a Train' and it is here that the album really breaks free, leaving virtually every other singer–songwriter album way back in its wake. It is a twin to 'LA Freeway', in being the second song on the side and having a big rolling melody that pulls at your heart. Like 'Texas – 1947', it concerns the young boy in Monahans, but this time he is not pulling a flattened nickel off the railway track, but accompanying an enigmatic old oil man around town who introduces him to his wizened friends as his 'sidekick'. Between the idolising boy and the "old-school man of the world", there's the potential for the story to turn mawkish, especially as the man approaches death, but Clark preserves the dignity of the old desperado as carefully as he guards the beauty of his own writing. This is a monster of a song, with pianos and acoustic guitars rising up for the biggest chorus on the album. It's a perfect tune and it's all Guy Clark – five tough and tender verses, a daring song subject, and a beautiful, climbing major-and-minor-chord melody.

With side one and side two mirroring each other, 'Like a Coat from the Cold' is the love song following 'Desperados Waiting for a Train', just as 'She Ain't Goin' Nowhere' follows 'LA Freeway'. Susanna Clark seems to be the subject of both songs, and where 'She Ain't Goin' Nowhere' catches her spirit, the lump-in-the-throat melodic descensions of 'Like a Coat from the Cold' catches the love. It's a song Clark has been defensive of, finding it too chivalrous, but he's being tough on himself. It's a beautiful song, from its grand first lines ("I've found comfort and courage / In bottles of whisky") to a chorus that is charming in its old-world gallantry:

But the lady beside me is the one I have chosen
To walk through my life like a coat from the cold

The modern world intrudes next, on what could be the album's most overlooked song, 'Instant Coffee Blues'. Clark moves the action masterfully, as a drifter (perhaps a songwriter?) gets picked up by a waitress and is taken back to her place. There are blurry recriminations in the morning – "'Man I was drunk,' she whispered in the shower" – but the instant-coffee blues blow away the awkwardness over the breakfast table as they chat and then part ways into the traffic of another day. Finally there is 'Let Him Roll'. You want something uplifting to finish? Or a farewell lullaby? You ain't going to get it. Instead comes the story of a "wino, tried and true" and his youthful, unrequited love for a prostitute in Dallas. The wino dies and "way off to the side" at his funeral is the now grey-haired woman "who turned his last proposal down in favour of bein' a girl around town". This provides a very suitable last chorus for the album:

Let him roll, let him roar
He always said that heaven was just a Dallas whore

And then there is the sound. Like a few other records that evoke a time and a place through a wondrous set of songs – comparable albums being Van Morrison's *Astral Weeks* or Dylan's *Blood on the Tracks* – *Old No. 1* has a distinctive sound that was never to be repeated. Acoustic and electric guitar, bass, piano, Dobro, pedal steel and harmony singers will all feature on other Guy Clark albums, and on countless other artists' records too, but the combination will never sound the same. It's to do with whatever particular magic was going on at RCA Studios in Nashville in 1975, and it's to do with the songs. They benefit enormously from the light-fingered production; in fact, they are freed by it, and so they breathe in every hesitation, fade on every poignant moment, and jump out for every chorus. Eight harmony singers are credited, but you barely notice them; there are seven guitar players, but every lick and guitar strum seems to ring clear. At the heart of the album is the singer–songwriter's guitar, the instrument all the songs stem from and around which all the other instruments fit and dance. *Old No. 1* is primarily an acoustic album, which further seals it at the heart of singer–songwriting, of which it is nothing short of a master class.

Buy it. Get it. No record collection complete without it. For those with the best of Springsteen or Lou Reed or Leonard Cohen in their minds and convinced the circle is closed and complete, *Old No. 1* has to be given a chance. You might not like it – there may be too much denim or mid-'70s grit, the musicians are called 'pickers' and it may all look and sound too much like country music. *Old No. 1* comes from that culture, but it also turns its back on it, going for something far more real and funky and moving. It is, in fact, more like a rock album or a West Coast singer–songwriter album, and if it had been marketed to those fields on its release, it might have gathered far more acclaim and sales. As it is, the flame is kept burning by a diverse group of admirers who see *Old No. 1* as a little like that train in 'Texas – 1947': coming out of nowhere, stunning those down by the tracks, before it disappears into the distance "like a mad dog cyclone".

Who Loves the Sun?

The Velvet Underground & The Go-Betweens

My first great realisation about The Velvet Underground was this: they were the first band I'd ever heard who wrote songs better than they could play them. Before the Velvets, almost every band I knew was more proficient on their instruments than they were at songwriting. The Velvet Underground changed this and, although I later came to appreciate their particular musical prowess, when I first heard them in 1975 I'd found a band that had managed to reverse rock history. No years of cover versions behind them. No neatly rounded Beatle-esque chords. But *songs*. And this is exactly what The Go-Betweens tried to do at the start: we wanted to be a band that wrote great songs – but could barely play them. This was partly due to our primitive musical ability, but also because to us it seemed noble and perverse – an attempt to upset the normal balance of rock 'n' roll between what songs you had and how good you were on your instruments. The kings and queens of this were The Velvet Underground.

An immediate pleasure of listening to the Velvets was that they took you into another world. Where other rock groups (always four or five men) offered songs, album covers and the odd interview about their back-story, the Velvets gave you much more. There was a woman drummer, an ice-cool German chanteuse and three very moody guys in sunglasses. Looming above and coming in waves from each album was New York. And above this, especially on the debut album *The Velvet Underground and Nico* (1967), there was Andy Warhol, the band's manager and producer.

Warhol was the key. He placed the Velvets in the middle of his whirl, joining them to an extraordinary group of people creating art and an equally extraordinary group of people living off the people who were creating art. It enriched the Velvets and enriched the experiences of those such as myself and fellow Go-Between Grant McLennan, who in Brisbane in the late '70s sought this band as inspiration – not only for their beautiful music, but for their collision with art, and thought, and energy, and groovy people. It was the glimpse of a life that helped obliterate the Brisbane of sunshine and beaches, offering instead darkness, ritual, cruel humour and songs. A dream world, you could say, for two Brisbane boys in search of a woman drummer.

Although Brisbane could never offer the cultural fix of Warhol's Factory, or even hope to approximate the roar and madness of mid-1960s New York, the idea that a band didn't have to be tied to music-making alone came to us from the Warhol/Velvets/Factory example. In 1978–79, The Go-Betweens abounded with projects that Grant and I wanted to build around the band. At this early stage of our career we even thought of the band as our calling card – the first thing to get us noticed – and then we'd incorporate filmmaking or book writing, or any other form of expression of which our young minds thought we were capable. So, around the release of our first single, 'Lee Remick' / 'Karen', we were writing a feature film script, planning and writing articles for a proposed fanzine, and starting our own record label, the Able Label, that our single came out on. It was a small 'factory' for sure, but busy, and based on the New York example we so admired.

And we weren't alone. Brisbane at the time was on fire. With the revolution of punk and post-punk crackling in the air – partly inspired by Brisbane band The Saints – there were groups of people pocketed around the inner city doing interesting things. Music had broken down the door and through it came artists, photographers, graphic designers and promoters who fed into the space that punk had made. There was a definite awakening, a new aesthetic that was influenced by the Velvets and Warhol. If punk was do-it-yourself culture, Warhol was the do-it-yourself man. He bought a camera and became a filmmaker, he got a rock group and became a record producer, he took photos from newspapers and made art. This was very inspiring in a town like Brisbane which, in the late '70s, had little-to-no arts infrastructure and gave minimal support to those attempting anything new.

Between us, Grant and I owned five Velvet Underground albums. There were the first four – *The Velvet Underground and Nico* (1967), *White Light/White Heat* (1968), *The Velvet Underground* (1969), and *Loaded* (1970) – plus a live album, *1969: The Velvet Underground Live* (1974). My favourites of these were the debut album (also the first one I'd bought), *Loaded*, with its peerless collection of rock songs, and the live double album, recorded in Texas, which captured the band in a clear, funky, low-key sound. I learnt from all three of them: from *The Velvet Underground and Nico* that pop ('Sunday Morning') could easily sit beside the experimental ('European Son'); from *Loaded* the wonder of the melodic power chord; and from the live album the beautiful, fragile sound that Grant and I tried to capture at rehearsal in our darkened lounge room in Toowong.

The Go-Betweens didn't play all that many cover versions live, so my memory of specific Velvets songs we did runs to just two – both performed under rather unusual circumstances. The first was in a hall in the outer suburb of Darra in the second half of 1978, at a gig ominously titled Operation Menace. The headline band was The Leftovers, and The Go-Betweens were the only support. The Leftovers had formed around the same time as The Saints. Musically they played an anarchic version of punk rock; in person they were the most terrifying band I'd ever been near. Real violence dripped off them, and they carried themselves as if to scare – not in a thuggish rock 'n' roll way, but in a quasi-passive, unpredictable manner that always put you on guard. They wore black, drove around in a long black Dodge, and came from Sandgate. That night there would have been only 40 to 50 people in the audience. We opened up with The Leftovers sitting on a table staring straight at us. Our first song? 'We're Gonna Have a Real Good Time Together' by The Velvet Underground, from the '69 live album.

The second occasion was a year later while we were rehearsing with our then drummer Bruce Anthon at his second-floor practice room in Adelaide Street in the city. There was a knock on the door and it was The Leftovers' bass player, Glen Smith, visiting with his girlfriend. Grant and I froze. Glen chatted with Bruce and then asked if he could play a song with us. We nodded as if our heads would fall off. He picked up an electric guitar and went straight into 'Run Run Run' by the Velvets. After finishing the song, he smiled and left. It was as if we'd passed some test. And what had brought together the town's toughest band and its wimpiest? The Velvet Underground.

The New York singer–songwriter Elliott Murphy, in his liner notes for the '69 live album, wrote: "What goes through a mother's mind when she asks her 15-year-old daughter, 'What's the name of that song you're listening to?' and her daughter replies: 'Heroin'?" This is similar to my first experience with the Velvets. It was in a suburban setting and I was 18 as I sat in my parents' lounge room with headphones on, listening to 'Heroin'. It didn't make me want to go out and buy the drug, but the music stunned and captivated me. As I sat there it was as if Lou Reed was whispering to me: "The chords to this song are just D to G, and that's all there is." The chords sped up, the chords slowed down, and nothing else happened. It was a eureka moment courtesy of The Velvet Underground. No embellishment was now needed – music could be naked and beautiful.

My own songwriting started soon after this. Before the Velvets, all music sounded complex to me. Heavy metal and progressive rock, the prevailing rock-music trends of the day, were centred on virtuosity and convoluted musical arrangements, both of which acted to cover or disguise the bones of a song to an extent that someone like me found intimidating and which left me unable to find a way in. My songwriting took the calm and clean melodic lines of the Velvets. As an influence, however, the lyrics of Lou Reed did present a problem: there were no drag queens in The Gap, no trashed amphetamine rich girls; I was too far from the New York demi-monde (we did have Sunday mornings, though). The lyric thrust I got came partly from Jonathan Richman and the Modern Lovers. They were a Boston band, and very big Velvets fans. Richman wrote about suburbia, and I could relate. It was an amalgam – of Velvets-inspired music and Jonathan Richman-style lyrics.

Trying to find information about Warhol and the Factory, especially when The Velvet Underground were around, was difficult. Now you can buy a book like Stephen Shore and Lynne Tillman's *The Velvet Years: Warhol's Factory 1965–67* (1995) and it's all there – the butcher-striped tops people were wearing, the wraparound sunglasses, the black leather boots, the silver foil on the walls, the stacked Warhol canvases in the background, and the Velvets practising. Joyous photos of John Cale looking impossibly handsome and smiling as he plays. Everyone in the book has some kind of charisma and, like Hollywood film stars, each knows the exact moment to turn and give the camera their best angle.

Somehow these photographs were available to us back then, but I don't know how that was. A book that I'm sure Grant and I had in the late '70s – Victor Bockris and Gerard Malanga's *Up-Tight: The Velvet Underground Story*, full of great Velvets/Factory images – I found out was not published until 1983. But at the time we knew the look and we thought the Factory was the most perfect rock 'n' roll environment of all time. Not much touring, hanging out in New York, fabulous parties, famous people and a place to write songs and practise. Who could ask for more?

The Velvet Underground is a feeling, a feeling that comes from their music and from their image. Has there ever been a band that sold so few records but was so well documented? You could almost call this The Velvet Underground's one piece of luck, in a career that offered few breaks and little fortune. The music lived on, as did the photographs and Warhol's film *The Velvet Underground and Nico* (1966). So you get both: the music, which is startling in its divorce from virtually all other '60s rock music (and remember this is a band from New York, not out in the woods), and a band that looks like no other '60s band, or any other band since.

One last lesson came from The Velvet Underground and it may be the most enduring. After the second Velvets album, John Cale was forced out of the band at Lou Reed's insistence. Cale and Reed had started the group and, through Cale's unorthodox instrumentation and Reed's street songs, laid the foundations of the band's sound. The music the Velvets made after this split was still grand, with no noticeable loss of song quality … but something was lost. Perhaps it was the idea of two artists working together, or the idea that a band should always hold on to the elements that make it the strongest. Whatever it was, Grant and I learnt from it, and gave each other room, while always believing in the common goal of our band. And later, when interviewers questioned us on how and why we still managed to work together over so many years, we'd quote Cale and Reed's split as a warning sign we'd heeded, as well as the desire to be as great as our favourite bands, one of which was certainly The Velvet Underground.

The Infinite

Tom DiCillo's *When You're Strange: A Film About The Doors*

The film starts with a smashed car in a ditch on a desert road. Out of the wreckage climbs Jim Morrison. The next scenes have him hitchhiking, and then suddenly he's in a car again driving through the desert; he turns on the car radio to hear an announcer bring breaking news: "Jim Morrison, the lead singer of The Doors, was found dead in his Paris apartment this morning." As the opening scene for a 'film about The Doors' it is disorientating and very strong – to have seemingly resurrected the group's lead singer and have him in a widescreen, real-life narrative hearing of his own death. Morrison keeps on driving and then the film cuts to a burning match. What we've seen is a cleverly manipulated use of footage Morrison shot with the film-maker Paul Ferrara back in 1969. The film they were making was called *HWY: An American Pastoral*; it is 50 minutes of loose, experimental film-making, typical of the late '60s, and has remained largely unseen for the past 40 years. The insertion of the announcement of Morrison's death into the soundtrack of the original film at the moment when he reaches for the radio is effective, but then *When You're Strange* loses its nerve. A kaleidoscopic rush of Doors images follows – some vintage surf footage indicates California, the band's birthplace; John F Kennedy sitting in the back seat of the Dallas cavalcade – while the narrator intones "The 1960s start with a shot", and we are firmly back in rock-documentary land.

When You're Strange returns at intervals to the *HWY* footage, but a context for its appearance is never established in the 90 minute run-through of the band's career. With the scenario of Morrison escaping from his own death forfeited, the film can only groove on the beauty of *HWY*'s desert landscape and the pleasure of seeing unknown footage of

Morrison in the last months when he was still lean and looking good in leather pants. What another director or documentary maker would have made of the footage is hard to guess. It is tempting to imagine Morrison's mysterious death and mystique, and the 50 minutes of film, in the hands of a more adventurous director such as Spike Jonze or Todd Haynes (who cast Cate Blanchett and Richard Gere as Bob Dylan in the 're-imagined' Dylan biographical picture *I'm Not There*), or even Quentin Tarantino. Where would they have taken the film? What trip would they have dreamt up with Jim at the wheel? They certainly wouldn't have circled back after such a promising start, as does director Tom DiCillo, because if any group can sustain a mind-bending ride of a film that pushes form and content way to the edge of what a rock-band documentary can be, then it's The Doors.

They were an LA band – no, they are *the* LA band – and every group that's followed them, be it Dream Syndicate, Guns N' Roses, Jane's Addiction or the latest hot band in their Silver Lake practice room striving for melody and meaning, is in their shadow. The Doors formed in 1965 and in the 72 months of their existence made six studio albums, of which three, *The Doors*, *Strange Days* and *LA Woman*, are rock classics. They were, crucially, a second-generation '60s band, and like The Velvet Underground in New York and The Great Society in San Francisco, their members set out to make music in late '65 that didn't emulate the British Invasion, in particular The Beatles, or electrify coffee-house folk roots into Folk Rock. Instead they invented the art-rock group, bringing to bear enthusiasms such as jazz and avant-garde music, film and literature, to shatter conceptions of what constituted a mid '60s rock band. The Doors could have made four fantastic low-selling albums like the Velvets, or imploded like The Great Society – that group's lead singer Grace Slick taking the very weird, self-penned 'White Rabbit' to her next band, Jefferson Airplane – if Jim Morrison hadn't asked each member of his band at an early rehearsal to bring a new song to the next practice session. Robby Krieger came back two days later with 'Light My Fire'.

There's a clip of it in *When You're Strange*, taken from *The Ed Sullivan Show*, and it's outrageous. Against a Technicolor studio set of lurid yellow and orange, Jim Morrison presents a vision of a lead singer that would shock and amaze today, were someone of his insolence and brilliance to be allowed anywhere near prime-time TV. He is in leather pants and jacket with a plunging white shirt, black shoulder-length curls, and nothing but intensity and concentration as he delivers a ferocious live lead vocal that leaves him spent and slumped in full-body close-up. He is 23 years old, and he'd been asked by Sullivan to omit the suggestive 'higher' from the line "girl, we couldn't get much higher", but he sings it anyway and that in part became the problem with The Doors. They kept having hit singles, but Morrison wasn't cut out to play the game. How much pop-chart success was factored in at the band's inception is hard to tell; presumably being able to get some good gigs and score any kind of record deal was then the limit of the dream. The explosion of 'Light My Fire' and the success of their debut album changed everything; a rock group as unusual, and as provocative, had never hit the number-one spot on the American charts before.

The tragedy of the band since their demise in 1971 is the extent to which Jim Morrison has come to dominate the legacy. On record and in the beginning they were four equals, with Morrison having to be at his best as a singer and lyricist to hold his ground. Footage of *The Soft Parade* recording sessions shows a lead singer as one part of a team, at times almost helpless as the others strive to make the album. The Doors were a great band, a unique constellation of musicians drawn together in a beautiful narrative (as all good groups are) and at a notable time – keyboardist Ray Manzarek and Morrison met at UCLA film school, guitarist Robby Krieger and drummer John Densmore at a pre-hippie LA meditation class. There's no bass player; Krieger, who is a flamenco prodigy, has been on electric guitar for just six months and plays with his fingers, Manzarek is into Bach and jazz, Densmore's drumming is percussive and dynamic, and the lead singer is a poet wanting to name the band after cherished lines from William Blake: "If the doors of perception were cleansed, everything would appear to man as it is: infinite." The wonder is that the band lived up to this; Morrison had a grand lyrical agenda but the rest of the group are also heroes, giving the standard rock-band format its first real shake-up and writing the music to a stable of songs that are strong and lasting.

When You're Strange has tacit support from the three remaining members of the group, although none is interviewed and there are no other contemporary interviews; the documentary relies on archival film footage, stills and a narration written by the director, Tom DiCillo, and read by Johnny Depp. The band has been burnt before by historical depiction, most noticeably in Oliver Stone's inaccurate and sensational biographical feature film *The Doors* (1991). DiCillo is obviously sympathetic to the group, and he has been given access to a bounty of quality, on- and off-stage footage – a happy outcome of Morrison's and Manzarek's film-school days. The director's intention is to closely weave The Doors' story and music into the social and political upheaval of the time. Yet making correlations and connections between music – lyrics in particular – and newsreel images is always hazardous, and this is borne out early when the first strains of 'Break on Through' are matched to a burning American flag. Later, in a live version of 'The End', DiCillo cuts from Morrison singing "I'll never look into your eyes ... again" to Martin Luther King's face in a newspaper on the day of his assassination, and then to Robert F Kennedy dying on the floor of the Ambassador Hotel – and though contemporary events can't be divorced from the work of artists as vital as The Doors, nor can they be linked to it as wildly as this. The questionable ability of the director to join lyric to image is further illustrated by his having weird clown faces and fairgrounds to illuminate 'People Are Strange', and, on the lyric "women are wicked", by cutting to a shot of a woman coyly taking off her bra and showing her breasts.

The strained literalism extends to the narration: Depp's voice-over is good and it's a pleasure to hear the inflection he brings to phrases such as "Bach-tinged blues runs" or his spooky reading of the Blake lines, but what can he do with sentences as fawning and banal as "It is music for the different, the uninvited. It carries the listener into the shadowy realm of dream" or "But if the band has a surreal fairground air, it is Morrison who is the frenzied trapeze artist"? The film does bring Morrison into focus, DiCillo seeing his rise and fall as the third great drama alongside the changing times and the band's unfolding career. What was Jim like? The film has two neat little exchanges. In one, Morrison does a belting, rasping vocal in a studio only to have someone off-camera advise him: "Don't overblow, Jim. You've got a long way to go." Smiling, he replies, "Why not?" In the other, a policeman asks him to stay in a limousine because there are too many people around the car. Morrison immediately gets out. He's the guy that can't say no, the person who'll always take the last drug and drink, the grinning daredevil. He's a rock god, but he's also recognisable as the friend you have who'll be the first to die.

And it's a depressing film. DiCillo stacks it with only the most confrontational and extreme footage of Morrison on stage. Given the nightmare of the newsreel images, the odd interspersions of the *HWY* footage, and the need to fast-track all of this into 90 minutes, it leaves little time to tell the tale of the joy and kicks of being in such an extraordinary band. There's always the music, though, and towards the end of the film comes the magic drift of notes heralding 'Riders on the Storm', as evocative and magical a seven minutes of music as has ever been committed to tape in the history of rock'n'roll. There is the soothing throb, the long gorgeous keyboard solo ... I see night-time beaches and the moon over the sea: everyone has a flicker sheet of images to this song. And DiCillo? Napalm, jungles on fire and screaming children. Break on through to the other side, man.

Tired and Emotional

Bob Dylan's *Time out of Mind*

He's in his mid-fifties. His last album of original material is seven years back. He thinks he might be through with songwriting. Then something happens; it might just be seven years of growing older, but new feelings come, and with them songs.

Every great Bob Dylan album has demanded a grand role from him. Some would call it the hero's role. All his '60s albums needed and had it. *Blood on the Tracks* has it with him as lover–confessor, *Desire* as mystic troubadour. Dylan is capable of writing great one-off songs, but an album full of them needs something more from him. It needs a role, shoes to step into, and when Dylan finds it he explodes. *Time out of Mind* is 72 minutes of relentless theme and brilliance. Maybe another 30 minutes of it exist somewhere that just didn't fit. For when Dylan's on fire, convinced he can spring songs from his current persona, then material is not a problem. It's just a matter of getting him into the studio and pressing 'record'.

Dylan's role on *Time out of Mind* is grizzled survivor. The women he once rhapsodised are now giving him trouble, the world looks way off-kilter, and generally he's "going down the road feeling bad". Whether this is how Dylan actually feels, it doesn't matter. There's a relish and hunger to get into every corner of what he sees that give the album the sense of being a very full portrait of him at the moment of recording. And this full portrait with information going right out to the edge is a characteristic found on all of his masterpieces.

Bizarrely, the album *Time out of Mind* most reminds me of is *Blonde on Blonde*. Both are long albums with big classic songs interspersed with blues, then topped with a long, hypnotic anthem at the end that you just can't believe is going to work but does. Both are big visions by a songwriter fully in control of his art, looking at a corresponding (love) life spinning out of control. In his mid-twenties Dylan met it with stoned befuddlement and French poetry; now it's midlife ennui and American hardboiled. Both times he nails it.

Two final things. The first is Dylan's singing. Those who don't like him often think he doesn't sing but talks. Those who like his singing often do because his singing has the rhythm and intimacy of talking. *Time out of Mind* seems very personal. It could just be the amount of humour and heartache on it, but the 'talking' hits me right in the ear. I follow Dylan through the whole album.

Finally, Daniel Lanois. Often maligned as producer. His detractors call his sound 'soupy'. *Time out of Mind* is his masterpiece. The splintered shards of reverb, half-buried keyboard lines, ringing guitars, all match and catch Dylan's grief. Listen to 'Love Sick'. Dylan is pulling shocks with the lyrics, but hear that upstroke guitar, hear the bang of the guitars before the chorus. Lanois shadows Dylan. You can't go back to something perfect, but Dylan's last two albums have 'sounded' poorer without him.

Going for a Song

Creedence Clearwater Revival's 'Have You Ever Seen the Rain?'

The merits of this song could have something to do with the circumstances of my first hearing it. In 1971, I convinced my parents to buy a record player. Before that, our house had little music save for the radio, which had increasingly caught my adolescent ear. My parents, with little knowledge of hi-fi and not much money, bought a blue all-in-one player that was light enough to carry with one finger. It had little-to-no power and the sound was tinny and high. But it was mine, and I was thrilled.

Soon after, my father came home from work and presented me with a stack of worn and scratched 45s. "These are for you," he said. A colleague of his at work had a part-time business in jukeboxes, and these records – my first – were the veritable workhorses sent out to graze after spending months or even years in service on jukeboxes in pubs and clubs around town.

I played all those that could still be played. Three stood out and they were all by Creedence Clearwater Revival: 'Green River', 'Who'll Stop the Rain' and 'Have You Ever Seen the Rain?' The last of these became my favourite. It was slower than the other two, and seemed to have a glory or majesty to its melody and lyric line that went straight to my heart. But beyond the genius of the song, it was the voice of its singer (and songwriter), John Fogerty, that really got to me. It had a size and force that took up all the space coming out of those tiny speakers. I was enthralled by it and would spend hours playing the record over and over again, digging the rasp, the croon, the side-of-the-mouth joy of his singing.

Listening to the record now, I hear the band more. The drummer,

Doug Clifford, and the bassist, Stu Cook, especially. What a rhythm section! They are high in the mix, bedrocking everything Fogerty has put into the song. Clifford is strong and steady, with great fills and accents around the chorus; Cook is warm and melodic. It's a surprisingly stripped-back sound, letting bass and drums lead, with all other instrumentation around the edges. And, of course, there's Fogerty. I love him as always, but I hear him in the picture – one part of the band.

And I remember the 13-year-old boy enthralled by this record. Miming to it in my parents' lounge, pretending that this lion's roar of a voice was coming out of my own throat. "I want to know," I'd sing, "have you ever seen the rain, comin' down on a sunny day?"

FICTION

The Coronation of Normie Rowe

I'd just returned from the pub and was reading on the couch when the phone rang. It was Normie's people, wondering whether I'd induct him into the Hall of Fame. The receiver felt heavy against my ear as I listened to their time and instructions. Eventually I said I'd get back to them, sometime soon, and later that evening, still on the couch, I thought about their proposal. And I thought of Normie. It could have been the fire, the third Scotch or the late-night reverie but it got my mind wandering, cartwheeling off, back to a time when we were all young and intent on making history.

It was 1966 and I was in London, a mod awakening to the coming dawn of psychedelia but resolute in my commitment to the chivalrous code of action and fashion. I had been in London only four months and already I was running faster, giddy, hitting gallery openings and foreign films and being sucked into the whispers of what not to miss before it became the next big thing.

Which is how I came to be at Otis Redding's first gig on English soil. The club was rammed with the crème de la crème of the British pop scene. Tom Jones. Chris Farlowe. Lulu. Paul Jones of Manfred Mann. Eric Burdon. All perched ringside, waiting for Otis to preach his testament of deep soul. I was against the back wall. My position in those days. I would have been high on Benzedrine, with a few rolled hash joints in my pocket and some Top 40 hit – Petula Clark's 'Downtown', say – echoing through my mind like a fairground parallax. I would have been cool. But then in a minute my cool would have been shattered. In walked Normie.

For a split second, in the time something can be pulled across your ears and you think you see something else instead, I thought it was Brian Jones of the Rolling Stones. It wasn't. Star power emitting from every pore. It was Normie and he looked magnificent, just how an international pop star should look in the summer of '66. Blond bangs. Caramel turtleneck. Checked hip-hugger trousers. Beatle boots. I bit on a cigarette and wondered what the hell he was doing here in London.

From 1964 to 1966 I had been in a Brisbane band called the Stig Mata Set. We started out as an R&B band, graduated to Who and Kinks covers, and then I began writing songs. We'd see Normie and his group The Playboys on the circuit, a mad rabbit-warren of clubs and halls with their background static of shrieking teenage girls, mod violence and maverick impresarios, cigar chompers some of them, who would work you three shows a night, months on end. It was fun. It was mad. And it all went by in a brilliant haze, innocent now, free as it was from dirty drugs and dirty denim.

Normie was king: of the charts, of the girls, of the whole damn thing. Even the blues boys admitted he had some voice. I got to know him backstage and at motel parties here and there, close enough for him to want to cover one of my songs, a thing called 'Don't Stay Angry at Me (for Long)', the demo of which, seldom played, remains one of my most prized possessions.

I grabbed him on Otis's last note. Undignified it was, but Normie didn't mind. He greeted me through the Brisbane fog of half a year ago. And said: "Mate, I'm recording tomorrow, come along." He scribbled an address on the back of my ticket stub and, like a pop star can, he popped a bubble – pricked it and vanished before my eyes.

I had been in some studios before, in Brisbane and in Sydney, but they were mud huts compared to what I was standing in now. This was a cathedral, situated halfway up Hampstead Hill. The musicians, London pros, were setting up as I got there; the usual configuration of drums, bass and guitar plus some cream you wouldn't see back in Australia. A percussionist, three girl singers, a keyboard player. Two guys huddled in the corner. The producers.

In the control room I found Normie holding a lyric sheet and singing softly to himself. Across the top was written 'Ooh La La'. I arched an eyebrow. "It's not bad," he said. Then the producers came over to run down a first take. Normie went into the recording room and I hung about in a far corner, trying to approximate a fly on the wall. There were sound adjustments and a last-minute sprucing of the arrangement and a check of who does what. The first notes of 'Ooh La La' started. Two and a half minutes later I was a mess.

I didn't want Normie to see me so I ducked out to a side room, 'Ooh La La' reverberating in my head. I was crying. I knew immediately what he'd done. This lone Australian boy had sung his guts out and accomplished something no Australian had done before. Whacked a big ballad with real soul. Climbed into it, through a hall of reverb and drama, and made a great record. A quick flash came to me – of his body jack-knifed round the microphone, arms flailing. I wiped the tears from my eyes and prepared a face to take back into that room.

"What do you think?" he shot at me.

"It's not bad." I said and he grinned. "Really great, Normie," I added and I could see that he knew I meant it.

"Think it will be a hit in Australia?" he asked.

The whole room exploded. One of the producers swivelled around: "I bloody well hope so."

We all knew a lot more was expected than that.
During the next few months he did gigs around London and I never missed a show. Our friendship didn't spill over into private time. We'd chat backstage, if there was one, or between sets, when he'd come over to my table and talk about the latest news from Australia, or the sad progress of 'Ooh La La' in England. He wasn't one to be bitter. That sunnyboy image he had with the broad toothy grin was what you got. So long as he had a band and a room to play in he didn't seem to mind. He also had stardom to go back to, when he needed a top-up of that. I came to think that London might even have balanced him, that it was good for him at this time of his life to shuffle through a crowd and not be torn apart.

I would take English friends to see him. They couldn't believe he wasn't a star. "A hit record!" I'd scream. "He needs a hit record!" It was a pleasure watching him in such small clubs. Back home I'd be pressed to the wall of some massive concert hall, girls screeching in my ear. Here I could dig him up close. The crowds were never big. His record company would drum up whoever they could: pop journalists, provincial DJs, minor celebrities. But there was no buzz. They needed a hit record.

Three months after 'Ooh La La' came 'It's Not Easy'. Same studio, same producers, same musicians – plus, for those who believe Normie never had the backing of his English record company, a full orchestra and a conductor. This time he was going for the big one. 'Ooh La La' had set things up and now all levers were pushed to ten. This was maximum drama, a big song from Cynthia Weil and Barry Mann that, inexplicably, no major artist had ever covered.

And Normie's vocal? Well this time I had my tears in check; emotions and admiration, though, still ran wild. His voice seemed to scale the treetops. Full of yearning, yet still holding every shred of pride. The musicians and conductor, hard nuts all of them, were blown away. But something was missing in the arrangement. The producers huddled. They didn't seem able to come up with anything. The clock ticked on the session. One last dollop of sugar was needed to send the song off into the stratosphere. But what?

"Can I try something?"

All heads spun towards me. I was Normie's mate, tolerated, but not expected to peep out an opinion.

"I've been singing along. Just give me a go at something. Please."

They looked at Normie. He hesitated.

"Let him have a go. He might have something." And then as I walked past: "Be quick."

I rushed into the recording room and jammed on Normie's headphones. The top of his range was C sharp. I had to hit an octave above it, and with a touch of soul. The track started. I coughed into the microphone and heard a canyon of reverb, so it was on. The chorus was about to come. A massive wave. I let the first half go and then, with my mind almost black, I pitched a midget's scream an octave up and sang the second half of the chorus with Normie. The song kept going. If I'd fucked it, they'd have stopped. Second chorus. Not black this time. I actually experienced it. Singing with Normie, hearing him as I did my part. The song broke down into cascading piano, timpani roll, the sea surge of the strings, the drums, and I wailed out the last chorus high above Normie.

Silence. The song was over. I looked through the glass into the studio. People were clapping. Two relieved producers were giving me the thumbs-up. I walked back a hero.

Occasionally when I'm driving from Launceston down to Hobart I'll hear it on the radio, and there I am. You can here me in the choruses. Sometimes I'll stop the car, other times I'll drive on. I'm very proud of it. And I think of all the songs I wrote, and all the effort and belief I put into bands, and I find the one thing that has lasted was this little piece of inspiration, done in London, so many years ago.

In 'Ooh La La' and 'It's Not Easy', Normie had his two guiding stars. His tragedy is that he didn't do a whole album in London. Whether it would have made any difference, at that moment in his career, is a moot point. But we'd have it. A big, cold, winter masterpiece, tanked on strings, choirs and heartbreak. And Normie's skyscraper voice, pleading with the angels. The producers and the musicians were there. The songs would have been found. The album cover? Well there is a photo in my collection, shot in London, in autumn, the last sunrays of the year falling on his face as he leans against a tree in a park. It wasn't meant to be.

'It's Not Easy' failed to chart and he was gone. Years later, some said that the demands from Australia were too great, that he'd had to go home and continue the pop-star rounds when what he really needed was more time in London. It should have been given. The prize was in view. But he was gone. I missed him, yet London was no sadder for me. By this time I was flying at a hundred miles an hour, my mod resistance to the coming tide of colour and strangeness overcome, and I was unravelling at the seams in a groovy way.

I lasted a few more years. The sight of me in 1970 was enough to scare the crows. It was my time to go. I bought the tea chests, filled the suitcase and was off again, to the next part of my journey, which would end 25 years later with my return to Australia.

And Normie? I kept an eye on him. Our paths crossed but our

fortunes had been reversed. The career path and survival prospects of a '60s pop idol always were shaky, at best, like walking across a goldmine on splintered boards. One day up, one day down.

The fire is dying now. I spread and dampen the embers with the poker. I think of the Hall of Fame, and I think of Normie. It can't be. He shouldn't be there. To me he's like one of those Siberian tigers. The ones with the white coat, the orange-and-black head and the thick, full fur. Suspicious, and magnificent in the wild. An animal always on the edge of extinction that you find only in the deepest Russian forest, or Las Vegas. That's Normie. I'll phone tomorrow. And say I can't do it.

Deep night, I shuffle off to the bathroom. I brush the teeth and look in the mirror. Straggly grey hair that I comb into place with my fingers. Fine lines around my eyes and mouth, and what is still, I believe, a fine face. I go down the hall to bed, books and an orange lamp ready to go. The wind is down now. I open the curtains and see blackness, not a house in view, just a single light on a neighbouring hill. I close the curtains and offer up a prayer.

It's not easy loving you, baby.

I don't see myself as an actual member of these bands. I'm more of a spirit; wishing to be in each of them has as much to do with location, history and haircuts as it does with the music each band made. Being in them transports me to their time and their magic, and looking at the list I see it is also a path, stopping just before what would be the eleventh band I wish I'd been in: The Go-Betweens.

Elvis Presley/Scotty Moore/Bill Black 1954

This puts me in at the beginning. I'm with Elvis, who already looks amazing, but who at the same time is putting himself together – discovering who he is. It's before 'Colonel' Tom Parker – it's still Sam Phillips, his secretary Marion Keisker (the secret heroine of rock 'n' roll) and Sun Studio. It's Memphis, of course, and the joint is jumping. There is great innocence everywhere. The music we are making no one can describe, which is always a good thing. The clothes we are wearing are absolutely outrageous. I follow Elvis around – it's pick-up trucks, clothes stores on Beale Street, the colours are pink, black, it's eyeliner, hours in front of the mirror on the hair, which is up, slick, with strands falling onto the forehead. Musically, we are the eye of the hurricane. Good music is around us on every corner: blues, gospel and Hank Williams/Snow country. We're feeding on it but we've made the break. We have hooded eyes and big smiles. No drugs, but uppers and a little beer. Elvis's mum is still alive, so all is right with the world. Memphis, 1954.

Buddy Holly and The Crickets 1957

Elvis in the desert. Lubbock, Texas: a dry, parched suburban scene to exotic Memphis. Buddy the suburban boy to Elvis's gloss-eyed southern belle. Songs as opposed to overt rhythm. Thirty hits in two years. The recordings are done in Clovis, New Mexico by Norman Petty. The studio has primitive, chunky, space-rocket gear – the recording room is the size of a closet. No buildings on either side of the studio, so you step out at night and see stars twinkling over the land. Lonely parking-lot rock 'n' roll. Yet 50 years later, after all the sonic improvements, two-inch tape and digital revolution, 'That'll Be the Day' will still hit harder, meaner and brighter than anything recorded since. The Beatles will follow, as well as The Velvets and The Modern Lovers, descendants of lonely strip, flat-running, suburban hiccuping garage-pop.

Peter, Paul and Mary 1962

I play chess in the Village, outdoors, while sipping high-octane espresso. I'm in a suit, have a small beard and an acoustic guitar. Here's the kick – I look like an advertising executive but I'm in the folk clubs playing amazing three-chord songs and singing about justice. Wild women and men are everywhere but no one is flashing any big signs, it's still all under wraps, what we are doing and what this scene is going to bust out into – the '60s – the counter-culture – but just whisper it, baby, it's still micro-cosmic. Just a few of us. Oh look, there's John Sebastian. And Mama Cass. And Paul Simon – all in rags. The '60s haven't broken yet but I can feel them coming. On weekends I drive up to Woodstock with friends and we talk politics, listen to Leadbelly and drink beaujolais in a wood cabin. Dylan nodded to me in the street yesterday. Dave Van Ronk gets me in a bear hug. And all the while I just chug along with my acoustic guitar hugged high to my chest, singing with those I love, knowing we're going to jump straight from Greenwich Village to the top of the charts in a year.

Question Mark and The Mysterians 1965

I imagine two conversations. Both occur anywhere in the USA in March, 1965. The first is between myself and my father, and takes place in the high-ceilinged lounge room of a big middle-class home in a 'good' suburb.

Me: Excuse me, Dad. I've just joined a musical group.
Father: (withdrawing pipe from his mouth) Well done, son. What is this musical group called?
Me: Question Mark and The Mysterians.
(A long unbroken silence follows …)

The second conversation is between myself and a young woman. I've always found her attractive, but she regards me as less appealing, and a little un-cool.

Me: Hi, Felicity. I've just joined a pop group.
Young Woman: (distracted) Um … oh … what's the group called?
Me: Question Mark and The Mysterians.
Young Woman: WOW!! That sounds incredible!!
(A very short silence follows …)
Me: Yeah, and we've just recorded our first single.
Young Woman: What's it called?
Me: (nonchalantly) '96 Tears'.

This is my favourite band name of all time. And it puts me in a mid-'60s garage band with one great song.

The Great Society 1966

It's San Francisco before it all goes really weird and mad. It's the golden moment before the invasion, when everyone is still friends and there aren't rock stars in the scene yet and no one is touring – just playing in ballrooms and houses and jamming and songs and jewellery and Victorian clothes and pot and fog and big houses on the sides of hills that are cheap and filled with good discovery and books and long hair for the first time. The Great Society are Grace Slick's band before she joins Jefferson Airplane but there is much more to it than that: they are an art band with Grace's husband, the filmmaker Jerry Slick, on drums and his brother Darby on guitar. Darby has just written 'Somebody to Love', and Grace has already written 'White Rabbit' – both are in The Great Society set played in small rooms to groovy fans. Grace and the songs will go on to the Airplane, but this year it's fresh and beautiful and new.

The Band 1967

The world around us is in flames. All we have is a pink house just outside of Woodstock. Albert got us up here. Said you've got to get out of New York, so we did – just in time. No LSD, just a jug and what's in the garden and some very strong coffee. Dylan comes around. He's the family man with young kids and a wife and he drives over most days just after lunch. We gather in the kitchen. Dylan says 'What?' after everything we say. Do you want to go down into the basement? 'What?' Do you want to play songs? 'What?' Do you have a guitar? 'What?' And then he starts to sing some of the most beautiful songs you've ever heard. Later all this will go sour. But for now we are smiling in every photo as we dance around each other with whatever instruments are to hand. We haven't made an album and we don't have a name and we're recording music with Bob Dylan that will never be released. And it's all true.

Gladys Knight and the Pips 1969

Big collars. The colours are brown, orange, purple and ripe yellow, the whacked colours of late-'60s American psychedelic television. I'm one of The Pips – off to the side of Gladys, who is doing the performance and who takes the pressure. The Pips are free, but drilled and slick. We spin, we turn, we break at the knees, we point, we bop, and then we come to the microphone and sing some outrageous lyric at exactly the right moment, and then we spin, and bring the knee up, and do a little shimmy at the side with our hands that tells you more about the story of the song. We can do 'rain' with our hands, we can do 'thunder' with our hips. The beauty of this whole thing is movement to music. Choreography for a TV studio or a club filled with the right people digging what we do, and knowing the glory and wonder of Gladys's voice, but appreciating The Pips, loving The Pips, as we shuffle and turn and spin, all together.

David Bowie and the Hype 1971

This is Bowie with cigarette holders and long hair. It's 12-string guitars, old pianos, hash, Velvet Underground records and all the pre-glitter debris of '60s London stewing in a house that Bowie and Angie and his bandmates and their partners dwell in – the beautifully named Haddon Hall. I come down the stairs from my upstairs room and Bowie is sitting cross-legged playing 'Quicksand'. While I am brewing tea in the kitchen and having my first cigarette of the day I hear him at the piano singing 'Oh! You Pretty Things'. I run my fingers through my soon to be shorn-off long hair and think: God, life can't get any better than this.

The Wailers 1972

It's big leaves and rich brown dirt, mountain tops with views down to crystal-watered bays – my view of Jamaica. Bob Marley and Peter Tosh, the Picasso and Braque of reggae. Two guys always sitting together with guitars, inventing, testing, searching, as they put a sound and a set of songs together. Gathering strands – weaving. A touch here, a touch there. Around them are paradise and poverty, a strange place but the right moment for their music. The two of them are happily building; it's the joy of collaboration, people around them are whispering – jealous or confused? What are the two of them doing? A distant volcano smokes, Marley grins, Tosh smiles – it's all invention to the sweetest of melodies.

Talking Heads 1975

There is paranoia on the streets. New York is still a dangerous city. Photos of inside and outside CBGBs look gas-lit. We are down from the Rhode Island School of Design with new designs on ... um ... rock 'n' roll. It's a beautiful sound, no clutter, spiky and melodic, and compact, just the three of us. This is before Jerry joins, so we sound like Buddy Holly or Elvis but a logical development, 20 years later. It is us against the world like the start of every great group. It's funky, too. The other bands on the scene don't know how to take us, especially when we load our gear neatly onto a hire trailer and drive away from the rock clubs. David has to get the trailer back to Midtown by midnight or we get docked 20 bucks. We need the money. We're running on ideas. And our music is a skeleton with each bone exposed, and we see beauty in this, we see something new, which is how we look, which is the torch we are taking to rock 'n' roll, which is a building, which is now on fire.